# GAME OF ENTREPRENEURS

## A GUIDE FOR START UPS.

DR. ABHISHEK VENKTESHWAR

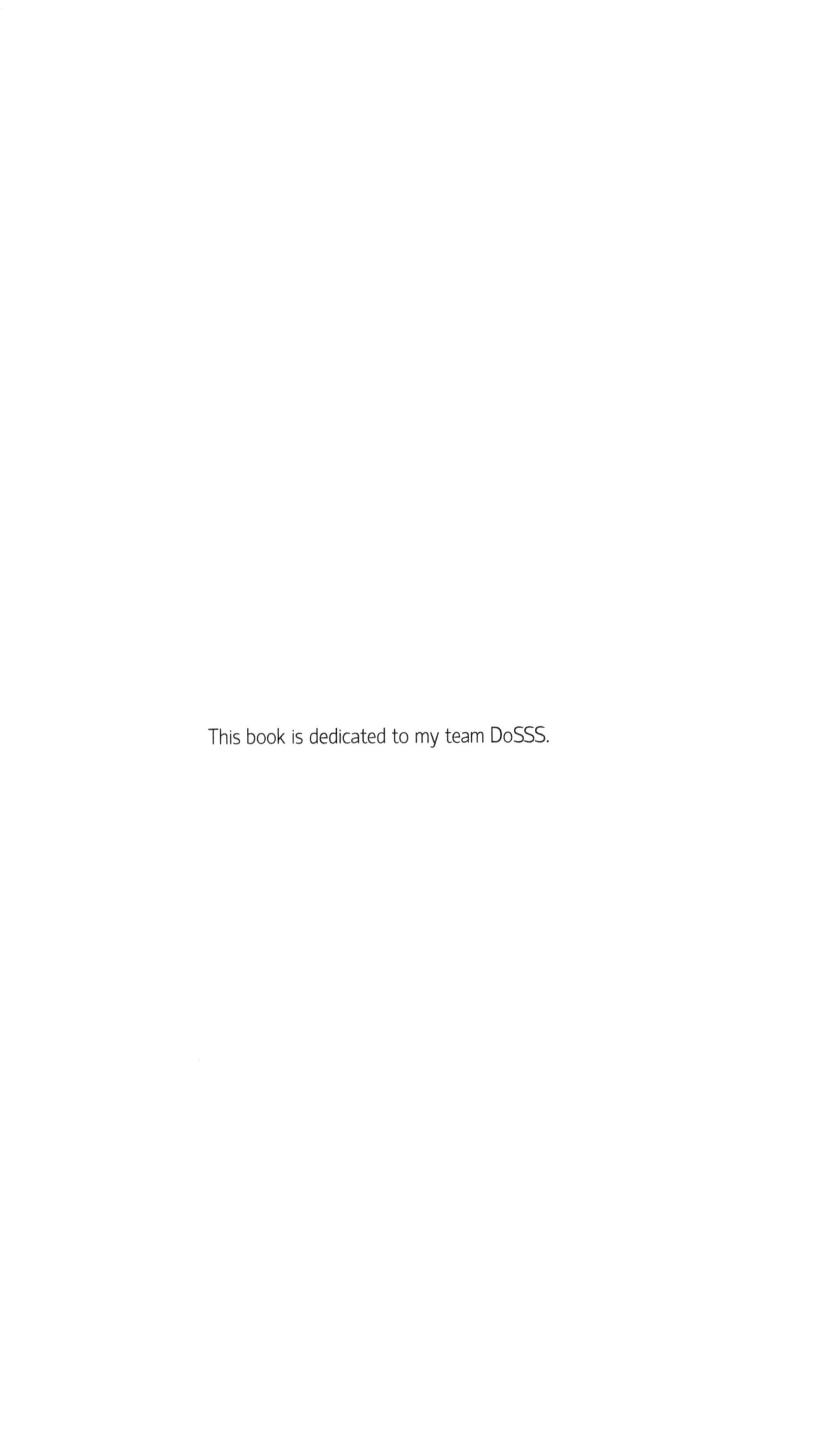

This book is dedicated to my team DoSSS.

# Contents

# Foreword

The concept of entrepreneurship is getting redefined in myriad ways. Be it the e-commerce platforms, services for cashless transactions or apps for education, new enterprises are witnessing a boom. Start-ups are making a huge impact on the global economy and India is one of the countries that has seen a massive spurt in their growth.

It has been estimated that 300 million people are poised to join India's workforce by 2040.Going by these statistics, we would need about 100 million jobs per year to accommodate the human resources. Are the existing big businesses capable of this feat? The answer is no. So where are we going to accommodate the huge chunk of people who would be ready to join the workforce? This is where entrepreneurship is playing a crucial role to create enterprises which in turn can employ people and use their skills productively.

While there are many enthusiastic aspirants who are keen to stake a claim at the altar of entrepreneurship, there is a common factor that at times prevent from launching commercially viable businesses. Most of the first generation entrepreneurs grapple with the nitty-gritty involved in setting up sustainable business.

The book *Game of Entrepreneurs* written by **Dr. Abhishek Venkteshwar** goes a long way in helping the aspiring entrepreneurs .Divided into six chapters, it is prolific and lucid at the same time .Dr. Venkteshwar has broken down complex systems and processes into the simple understandable concepts. Right from the basics of setting up a business to factors underlying business process outsourcing. The book is a real gem for those intending to gain insight into entrepreneurship. Each chapter in the book comes with case studies, providing experiential evidence and clarity to the readers. The chapter such as Entrepreneurial Strategies and Change Leadership provide a new perspective into launching and running of an enterprise. In the chapter Succession Planning for Entrepreneurs, Dr. Venkteshwar has deftly tackled one of the serious concerns for any enterprise-grooming the second line of command.

It is also my belief that entrepreneurship and education need to go hand in hand. Programs structured to help aspirants understand the nuances of business can go a long way in nurturing entrepreneurs. Prof Venkteshwar's book is a valuable addition towards this. All the chapters are strategically planned to provide a strong foundation to establish a successful start-up. I strongly feel that this book will prove to be a boon to those who are searching for an authoritative voice on entrepreneurship in simple, clear tones.

**Dr. Kiran Maney**

# Preface

It's true that entrepreneurs can have a significant impact on society, both by creating wealth and by introducing innovations that improve our lives. Understanding the fundamentals of starting and running a business, as well as effective advertising techniques, can be essential for success in this field. Additionally, change leadership and succession planning are important considerations for the long-term sustainability of any enterprise. It's great to see a comprehensive resource like this available to students interested in pursuing entrepreneurship.

# About The Author

Dr. Abhishek Venkteshwar

Dr Abhishek Venkteshwar is currently the Assistant Director-Student Activities & Events, and Assistant Professor in Alliance School of Business at Alliance University. He previously worked as an Assistant Professor at Jain University-CMS and then was promoted as Head-Program Development & Student Affairs , Knowledgeum at the Jain Group. Dr. Abhishek is also a Subject Matter Expert for International Business at UpGrad Campus. Dr. Abhishek headed the spectator engagement in Khelo India University Hames 2022. His Educational qualifications include D.Lit (HC), PhD, M.Phil , PGDUT,UGC-KSET, MBA and B.Sc (Hons). He is the recipient of three gold medals for Academic excellence and completed a course in University Teaching from the University of Newcastle, Australia. He is also a certified awarder by The Duke of Edinburgh Awards, UK. Dr. Abhishek has been certified by Harvard University, Yale University, IIM-Bengaluru and ISB Hyderabad. In his career span of 10 years, he has authored more than 67 papers in several UGC care/ Scopus indexed international journals with over 100 citations on google scholar. Dr Abhishek has authored/co-authored over 22 text books in various management disciplines. Dr Abhishek is a Reviewer in Asia Pacific Management Review, Elsevier. In the year 2020, he was awarded the "Best Professor" by RULA International Awards, Global Leadership Awards and DR Research Awards making it a hat trick. In 2022, he was awarded the Global Best Teacher Award, one of the most prestigious international teaching awards. Dr. Abhishek has been a panellist on several TV shows including Republic and News 9. He follows a 3 E Approach to University Teaching - Education, Engagement and Entertainment. He has observed that 90% of the learning happens in the engagement phase and therefore developed a unique pedagogy titled "Game of Cases", which is a unique blend of traditional teaching, case simulation, academic activities and stress busters with extensive use of social media. This has worked wonders for his students, and he is constantly looking for opportunities to enhance his skills.

# Acknowledgements

This book has been a gratifying experience in my academic journey.

I would like to thank the Chancellor Prof Premanand Shetty, Pro Chancellor Mr. Abhay Chebbi, Vice Chancellor Dr. Anubha Singh , Pro Vice Chancellor, Student Administration and Affairs Dr. Punith Cariappa , Pro Vice Chancellor, Banking, Finance, Development and New initiatives Mr Prakash S Budur , Registrar Dr. Nivedita Mishra , Registrar (E&E) Dr Ajay Kumar Yadav of Alliance University for their unconditional support.

I am indebted to Dr. Punith Cariappa for inspiring me to author this book.

I also take this opportunity to thank the Director Dr. Patial, Executives Mr. Balaji, Mr. Harish and Mr Manoj of the Department of Student Support Services, AU for constantly supporting me in this journey. I would also like to thank the student interns Mr. Rakhsit, Mr. Ajay, Mr. Krishna, Ms Hirmanyi and Ms Sudhiksha for motivating me to write this book.

I must take this opportunity to thank my mother Ms Meenakshi,who has been the guiding force in my life and has stood by me through thick and thin.My heartfelt gratitude to my late father Mr Venkteshwar , grandparents Ms Indira Shanmugam , Ms Shymala Vinayakam, and Mr Shanmugham. I would also like to express my gratitude to my family Ms Nirupa and Ms Anjali .I should not forget to thank my confidante Ms Geeta Samant, who has been a rock in my life.

Finally, I am sincerely obliged to all those who have directly or indirectly helped me in the completion of this book.

**Dr. Abhishek Venkteshwar**

# SETTING UP A BUSINESS

**Business**

Businesses are activities that provide goods and/or services in exchange for money or other goods and services.

A variety of businesses contribute to our local economy.

These include:

- Designing (buildings, gardens, paths, posters, etc.)
- Manufacturing or producing (goods like clothing or furniture, or parts of goods to be used by others to make complete goods, such as processing paper to make books
- Supply and distribution (moving goods from producer to client)
- Selling (retailing – buying from a producer or another intermediary business and selling to the consumer, or wholesaling – buying from a business and selling to other retailers or repair businesses
- Installing (fitting or connecting the product to the customer's home or business)
- Repairing (restoring broken or defective goods to working order)
- Service industries (tourism, information and communication services, leisure activities, etc.).

**Entrepreneur**

An entrepreneur is someone who starts or operates a business venture and assumes the responsibility for it. He or she provides goods or services to individuals or businesses for payment.

Some personal qualities entrepreneurs have include

- Curiosity and creativity

- Motivation and self-confidence
- Willingness to take riskseagerness to learn
- Ability to co-operate
- Ability to identify opportunities
- Ability to innovate (do something that nobody has done before) and lead
- Determination to overcome obstacles ('never take no for an answer!')
- Ability to learn from mistakes made by oneself and others, etc.

These qualities help the entrepreneur to think, analyze, solve problems and take action. Not every entrepreneur will have all of the above qualities. Many of these qualities are latent within us and we may not even be aware that we possess them. They can also be acquired through the learning process.

## 1. DEVELOPING MY ENTREPRENEURIAL SKILLS

People who start their own business have control over what they do in their working life. By managing their own business, they have the opportunity to shape their work environment and make an impact on their community. But often there will be resistance, especially if a new business idea is introduced. Therefore, one needs management skills to make the business successful as well as to convince the community that it can only help them, or at least can do them no harm

A good manager is a planner, a person who has vision, sets goals for achieving that vision and ensures that the necessary resources, financial and human, are obtained and allocated in time.

**Some key qualities good managers have:**

- Reliably
- Integrity (financial and ethical)
- Ability to lead
- Ability to set a goal and work towards it in small steps
- Eagerness to meet obligations, etc.

**Communication**

Good communication in business is important, because clients and business partners need to understand precisely what you are trying to buy or sell. Businesspeople need to be cheerful, keen, polite and helpful. Entrepreneurs should show interest in the customer and listen carefully to find out as much as possible about his or her needs. Listening is an important part of communicating.

- The entrepreneur needs to inform clients and business partners about the products and/or services they are selling and how these can meet their needs. Being honest and frank about our product or service can help build clients' trust and confidence in us. This means that we should not give the client an incorrect impression of our product. Being frank in general may also help us to buy materials or services at a reasonable price from our business partners.

**Time Management**

- Managing time is an essential part of good business planning, because time is a resource that has a monetary value. Poor time management usually leads to last- minute rushes to meet deadlines, causing stress and inferior performance. This may result in a product or service of poor quality and/or it not being delivered in time. A disappointed customer may seek a more reliable business provider.

**Time should be allocated to tasks depending on:**

- When the product or service is to delivered?
- How long the preparation of the product or service is likely to take?
- The need to co-ordinate people working on the product or service preparation
- How important the product or service and the client are to the business as a whole?
- Good time management allows for contingencies beyond our control, such as bad weather.
- Often, we must undertake several tasks at the same time in order to complete our job. We do this by estimating the amount of time necessary for each task and organizing our work accordingly. This is true of many of the activities that we take on in our everyday lives. For example, when

we cook we do not prepare one dish after another. Rather, we carry out our chopping, mixing and boiling up in such a way that all our dishes are ready to serve up just when we want them.

- Similarly, a person working on a task may be asked to help with another task when the work situation requires it.
- The time taken for the various stages of production should be recorded, so that clients can be given estimates of delivery time and the timeframe of future projects may be planned.

## Practicing Business Ethics

- Businesses need to function according to established law and rules set out by the community as well as the prevailing ethical standards . Investors, lending institutions and customers pay close attention to the standards of practice of businesses. But most importantly, young entrepreneurs may wish to set their own high ethical standards.
- In addition, many groups of businesses have established ethical standards for specific businesses. These standards of practice are a core set of values, developed by that group of businesses that govern the relationships between business and customers. Although they are not legally required, these values help to provide levels of service that distinguish the best businesses and build confidence among clients.

## Encourage them to think of issues surrounding:

- Conflict of interest
- Corruption and bribery
- Environmental responsibility
- Non-discrimination against others, for instance women, people with hiv/aids
- And people with disabilities
- After-sales service
- Truthful advertising
- Fair treatment of staff
- Refusal to deal with illegal partners, etc.

## Matching my skills with business

We all have skills that we use in day-to-day life. We can use some of these skills (or a combination of them) to launch a viable business.

**Types of Skills:**

- Thinking (being creative, solving problems, making decisions, observing my surroundings, basing actions on needs and opportunities of the immediate context, etc.)
- Conducting myself (believing in myself, managing my life, being responsible, etc.)
- Interacting with people (working with others and accepting others irrespective of their cast, gender, social status, whether they have a disability or not, etc.)
- My safety and survival (hiv/aids prevention, self-preservation, first aid, drug abuse prevention, etc.)
- What i can do (repairing bicycles, cooking, making crafts, reading, singing, etc.).

The skills that will help us in business are likely to be a combination of our personal (entrepreneurial) qualities and our technical knowledge and expertise acquired in school. Our skills should not be confined to traditional stereotypes. For example, girls may make good motor mechanics.

## 3. ENTREPRENEURIAL PROCESS

Personal attributes are the characteristics of entrepreneurs that make them different from non-entrepreneurs. This theme has been fertile in research into entrepreneurship. In looking to contribute to the identification and understanding of the behavior that may lead an entrepreneur to success, studies by McClelland (1965) set forth the following entrepreneurial characteristics:

- Seeking opportunities and initiative,
- Identification of opportunities,
- Ability to react to frustration and 'stressing' situations,
- Demand for quality and efficiency,
- Commitment,
- Establishing goals, planning and systematic monitoring,
- Persuasion and a network of contacts, and

- Independence.

Timmons (1978) agrees that certain personal attributes, such as the need for realization, a propensity for taking calculated risks, and control locus (an intense desire to be in control of one's own destiny), are observed in the majority of successful entrepreneurs.

The importance of human factors is also reinforced by Beugelsdijk and Noorderhaven (2005), who conducted empirical research with 14,846 individuals in Finland and showed that entrepreneurs differ from the general population, and with wage- and salary earners, in a number of characteristics, particularly in individual responsibility and effort.

Filion (1999) has stated that the literature often points out that entrepreneurs actively strive to achieve goals, and that they develop tenacity and creativity, as well as the ability to detect opportunities and that they are agents for change, that is, they do new and different things.

Salim (2004), in his turn, emphasizes that the successful entrepreneur has the following characteristics: takes risks, identifies opportunities, understands the business field, is organized, makes correct decisions, possesses leadership skills, is dynamic, is independent, is optimistic and has good business sense.

Dornelas (2001) adds to these attributes dedication, seeking wealth, planning, value to society and a forward-looking vision.

Clercq and Arenius (2003) state that there is a relation between human capital, i.e., the experience and understanding of the entrepreneur, and the success of the entrepreneurial activity, so that those who are best educated and invest more resources in improving their abilities are more apt to reap the benefits through their entrepreneurial activities.

Bygrave (2004) on the other hand, affirms: "We know that there is no neat set of behavioral attributes that allow us to separate entrepreneurs from non-entrepreneurs". Meanwhile, he emphasizes that "it does appear that entrepreneurs have a higher locus of control than non-entrepreneurs, which means that they have a higher desire to be in control of their on fate". Instead of using psychological terms to describe the entrepreneur's characteristics, Bygrave (2004) uses a set of everyday words, which he named "The 10 Ds":

## 4.  THE 10 D'S OF ENTREPRENEURSHIP

1. **Dream**- Entrepreneurs have a vision of what the future could be like for them and their businesses. And, more important, they have the ability to implement their dreams.
2. **Decisiveness** -They do not procrastinate. They make decisions swiftly. There swiftness is a key factor in their success.
3. **Doers**- Once they decide on a course of action, they implement it as quickly as possible.
4. **Determination**- They implement their ventures with total commitment. They seldom give up, even when confronted by obstacles that seem insurmountable
5. **Dedication**- They are totally dedicated to their business, sometimes at considerable cost to their relationships with their friends and families. They work tirelessly. Twelve-hour days and seven-day work weeks are not uncommon when an entrepreneur is striving to get a business off the ground.
6. **Devotion**- Entrepreneurs love what they do. It is that love that sustains them when the going gets tough. And it is love of their product or service that makes them so effective at selling it.
7. **Details** -It is said that the devil resides in the details. That is never more true than when starting and growing a business. The entrepreneur must be on top of the critical details.
8. **Destiny** -They want to be in charge of their own destiny rather than dependent on an employer.
9. **Dollars**- Getting rich is not the prime motivator of entrepreneurs. Money is more a measure of their success. They assume that if they are successful they will be rewarded.
10. **Distribute**- Entrepreneurs distribute the ownership of their businesses with key employees who are critical to the success of the business. Note. Source: Bygrave, W. D. (2004). The entrepreneurial process. In W. D. Bygrave & A. Zacharakis (Eds.). The portable MBA in entrepreneurship (p. 6).. Hoboken, NJ: John Wiley & Sons.

Bygrave (2004) observes they are the external influences surrounding the beginning of the business and its development. He underlines the influence the local environment has on the willingness of the entrepreneur to open a business. He refers to Silicon Valley, where a set of favorable conditions, such as support from public policies, proximity to universities, access to technology and availability of financial resources combine to make this a good location for new ventures. Environmental factors also include sociological factors such as: role models, family responsibilities, the trade-off between the experience that comes with age and the optimism and energy of youth, and contacts (a network of personal relationships).

## 5. UNDERSTANDING THE COMPETENCIES OF THE ENTREPRENEUR

Based on the professional trajectories of highly successful entrepreneurs, Nassif et al. (2004) developed a diagram that presents two dimensions to accommodate the competencies extracted from empirical research: the affective and cognitive dimensions. They also identified other variables, which have been categorized as environment, individual values and results.

In their research, the authors verified that: Despite being fragmented in the theory on entrepreneurship, the affective and cognitive dimensions are not dissociable in practice; The affective aspects appear with greater intensity and frequency in field research into entrepreneurship, despite a tendency in the literature on this subject to value the cognitive aspects more highly; . In the literature dealing with entrepreneurship, there is a strong emphasis on knowing how to do and not on knowing how to act. However, the research shows the importance of the person and his/her trajectory, intentions, world vision, values, beliefs... that is, on knowing how to be; . As such, the integration and harmonization of the affective and cognitive dimensions becomes necessary because treating them separately can generate unsatisfactory results.

The diagram developed by Nassif et al. (2004) contributes to the understanding of the entrepreneurs by categorizing their characteristics in dimensions that are related to affectivity and cognition. These dimensions constitute the pillars of the author's diagram, which also frames a static perspective.

### CASE STUDY
### ZOMATO: AN INDIAN STARTUP ACQUIRING THE WORLD

Zomato, an online restaurant guide, is one of the fastest ways to search places to eat around you. It is currently serving 22 countries worldwide and covers more than 1 million restaurants. Initially known as Foodiebay, this successful Indian startup was started by IIT graduates Deepinder Goyal and Pankaj Chaddah in 2008. Zomato has its headquarters in New

Delhi. In June 2010, it expanded its reach to Pune and Bangalore and then to Chennai, Ahmedabad and Hyderabad in 2011. In a very short span of time, Zomato went global and started providing its services in Dubai in September 2012. Later, it expanded to United Kingdom, Sri Lanka, Qatar, Philippines, South Africa, Turkey, New Zealand, Brazil, Indonesia and Portugal.

In November 2014, Zomato raised $60 million funding from its biggest shareholder Info Edge (India) Ltd , Vy Capital. Existing investor Sequoia Capital values the firm at $660 million.

Since July 2014, Zomato has acquired seven companies in various parts of the world to extend its reach in the restaurant search space and the biggest one being of Urbanspoon which has been a dominant player in the US, Australia and Canada. In April 2015, Zomato acquired MapleGraph, a Delhi-based startup and built a cloud-based point of sale product for restaurants known as Maple POS which was later renamed to Zomato Base. It has restaurant features such as menus and inventory management and has a built in payment solution to accept credit and debit card payments. The company also acquired US based Next Table which is a restaurant reservations and table management platform.

The collaboration of Zomato with travel itinerary planning portal TripHobo allow users to access content and deals on restaurants in addition to itinerary based recommendations. The launch of Zomato for Business application has helped business owners to engage with customers to drive business. Zomato's entry in food ordering space is likely to affect Foodpanda and TinyOwl's business in Mumbai

Apart from listing and reviews, Zomato will now own the communication channel between hotels and customers via online ordering and table reservations.

As the company is going more and more global, it rebranded its logo that so that it could transcend cultures, languages and geographic boundaries.

**Objectives:**

- To expand across the globe as a leading service provider

- To increase their fund and revenue

- To own the communication channel between the consumer and the businesses

**Strategies Adopted:**

Zomato uses different platforms to engage their customers with them. It is one of the finest brands in terms of social media marketing.

**Facebook:**

Images play a very important role in social media marketing. The images posted on Zomato's facebook page are very entertaining and each post marks excellence and higher degree of creativity. They create something for ongoing events. One cannot miss the posts which are simple yet engaging. They prefer quality to quantity.

**Twitter:**

The Foodie Friday contest received a great response on Twitter.

**Instagram:**

It lets people share the foodie photographs by using the tag #zomato and the image automatically gets shared on the microsite.

Zomato also chose **Mobile Marketing** to reach their customers which took the compnay to a different level.In the initial phase, it was just a website which displayed number of restaurants, revenues and recommendations. Then the company came up with the decision to have a smartphone based application and Zomato application was developed and made available for Google Android operating system. Later it launched applications for Windows phone, IOS and BlackBerry devices.

The Zomato's application help users to follow updates on their favourite restaurants, follow other reviewers and friends and create wish lists. The users get notifications for any new reviews added by other users, ratings as well as menu along with the some pictures .The users can also invite friends to follow them and their activities on Zomato.

The company started food delivery in NCR in April 2015 and users had an option to order food from restaurant using the main application. After a month, Zomato has now unbundled the feature and has launched a separate application – Zomato Order, which will be opening up for Hyderabad, Mumbai, Bangalore, Kolkata and Pune.

**Results Achieved:**

- Zomato has more than 159k followers on twitter and there is a huge customer engagement on facebook with more than 12,07,000 likes.

- 50% of Zomato's 30 million plus monthly visits come from its mobile application across the globe

- The company is now planning to expand its business and is aiming to launch in 15 more countries in the next year or so.

**Learnings:**

When it comes to restaurant search and discovery, Zomato is indisputably the leader. It has experienced phenomenal growth in recent years. Zomato knows its audience and it has used the right approach to engage with them through their marketing strategies. It has been constantly evolving around user experience.

# CHAPTER TWO

# ENTREPRENEURIAL STRATEGIES

## 2.1 INTRODUCTION TO STRATEGY

Strategy is a broad concept that covers a multitude of different issues, concepts, and methods. Many topics are considered in the formulation and implementation of strategy including industry analysis, competitors analysis, ethics, strengths/weakness, value creation, technology, innovation, product development, diversification, balancing the needs of various stakeholders, strategic alliance, organizations design, virtual organization, reward system, corporate cultures and corporate governance.

Every business organization of all sizes must prepare for an increasingly complex future, companies must deal with variety of strategic, technological and organizational forces on a daily bases. All these forces work together to redefine the economics and competitive landscape of the industry. Forward looking firms will seek to create new sources of competitive advantage by participating and shaping how industries evolve in the times ahead. Yet some challenges also threaten to erode the long held competitive advantage of companies that are slow to react or unable to mount an effective response.For practicing managers and leaders, strategy is at the center of the effort to create value for customers, to respond to competitive challenge, and to build strong organizations.

Globalization has become etched in our competitive landscape, including new opportunities and threats from emerging and developing countries that are fast becoming vibrant competitors. Companies are continuing to innovate breakthrough products and services and technologies to serve customers at ever faster rates. They are planning and organizing their activities using new methods, techniques and modes of operations, especially with the pervasiveness of the Internet and the rise of 'virtual' ways of doing the things. They are reaching to new customers in new parts of the world they never previously entered.Today all firms will necessarily compete with each other in the same way. Each firm is likely to devise its own strategy to deal with its competitive rivals to serve its particular base of customers, and to act on the changes that impact the way it operates. Each firm needs to develop a competitive advantage in its strategy that enables it to compete effectively.

Strategy refers to the ideas, plans, and support that forms employs to compete successfully against their rivals. Strategy is designed to help firm to gain an edge over its rivals which generates successful performance over an extended period.

## I. Definition of strategy:

- James.B.Quinn "Strategy is a pattern or plan that integrates an organization's major goals, policies, action sequences into a cohesive whole."
- William Gluick" Strategy is unified comprehensive and integrated plan designed to ensure that the basic objective of the enterprise are achieved."
- Henry Mintzberg" Strategy represents a fundamental congruence between external opportunity and internal capacity. It is a pattern in a stream of decisions and action"

## I. Features of Strategy

- The process of strategy formulation results in no immediate action.
- Therefore, strategy must next be used to generate strategic projects through a search process.
- Thus, strategy becomes unnecessary whenever the historical dynamics of an organization will take it where it wants to go (when the search process is already focused on the preferred areas).
- Strategy formulation must be based on highly aggregated, incomplete and uncertain information about classes of alternatives (at the time of strategy formulation it is no possible to enumerate all the project possibilities which will be uncovered).
- Successful use of strategy requires strategic feedback.

- Since both strategy and objectives are used to filter projects, they appear similar. However, they are distinct. Objectives represent the ends which the firm is seeking to attain, while the strategy is the means to these ends.
- Strategy and objectives are interchangeable; both at different points in time and at different levels of organization. A typical hierarchical relationship results: elements of strategy at a higher managerial level become objectives at a lower one.
- Strategy is not response to short-term fluctuations in operations or the environment, nor is it the response to the frequent short-term reports on, for example, sales, labor turnover, weekly output, or competitors' prices that every manager receives.
- Strategy is not a set of numbers merely projected out three to five years; it is not an extrapolation exercise based on this's years balance sheet and profit-and-loss statement. Rather, the emphasis in strategy is on the quality and texture of the business.
- Strategy is not a rationalization of what we did last year or of what appears in next year's budget. An actual strategy, in contrast, as a longer-term plan that set the direction and tone of the shorter- range plan.
- Strategy is not a statement of pious intentions or optimistic wishes. Instead, a strategy must identify ways by which at least some form of superiority over competitors is to be achieved.
- Strategy is not a cluster of ideas in the minds of a few select leaders of the company - ideas labelled strategy if and when they are voiced because they come from key individuals. Rather, the concepts are disseminated and understood by all managers to at least the middle levels of the organization and perhaps below.Above all, strategy is an expensive process both in terms of money and managerial time.

## III.  5P's of Strategy

Mintzberg first wrote about the 5 Ps of Strategy in 1987. Each of the 5 Ps is a different approach to strategy. They are:

- **Strategy as a Plan:** Planning is something that many managers are happy with, and it's something that comes naturally to us. As such, this is the default, automatic approach that we adopt – brainstorming options and planning how to deliver them.

- **Strategy as Ploy**: Mintzberg says that getting the better of competitors, by plotting to disrupt, dissuade, discourage, or otherwise influence them, can be part of a strategy. This is where strategy can be a ploy, as well as a plan.For example, a grocery chain might threaten to expand a store, so that a competitor doesn't move into the same area; or a telecommunications company might buy up patents that a competitor could potentially use to launch a rival product.

- **Strategy as Pattern:** Strategic plans and ploys are both deliberate exercises. Sometimes, however, strategy emerges from past organizational behavior. Rather than being an intentional choice, a consistent and successful way of doing business can develop into a strategy. For instance, imagine a manager who makes decisions that further enhance an already highly responsive customer support process. Despite not deliberately choosing to build a strategic advantage, his pattern of actions nevertheless creates one.

- **Strategy as Position:** "Position" is another way to define strategy – that is, how you decide to position yourself in the marketplace. In this way, strategy helps you explore the fit between your organization and your environment, and it helps you develop a sustainable <u>competitive advantage</u>. For example, your strategy might include developing a niche product to avoid competition, or choosing to position yourself amongst a variety of competitors, while looking for ways to differentiate your services.

- **Strategy as Perspective**: The choices an organization makes about its strategy rely heavily on its culture – just as patterns of behavior can emerge as strategy, patterns of thinking will shape an organization's perspective, and the things that it is able to do well.For instance, an organization that encourages risk-taking and innovation from employees might focus on coming up with innovative products as the main thrust behind its strategy. By contrast, an organization that emphasizes the reliable processing of data may follow a strategy of offering these services to other organizations under outsourcing arrangements.

## IV.  Forms of Strategy

- **Intended strategy**: It is a corporate level strategy in which organizational decisions are determined only by analysis, for various reasons the intended strategy hardly survives in its original form. Unforeseen environmental developments, resource constraints, will result in some parts of the intended strategy being unrealized.

- **Deliberate strategy:** Strategist will want to take advantage if new opportunity presented by the environment even if it is not the part of intended strategy, they are secondary set of plans to support and maneuver the intentions. For eg, when government gave subsidies for solar power generations, many business have increased their investment and hiring in this sector.
- **Emergent strategy:** The complete new strategy or changes in the existing strategy because of unforeseen events in the external environment can be termed as emergent strategy. For eg: to avoid the saturated markets in the cities for Flat tvs Toshiba concentrated to increase sales in rural markets of India.
- **Realized strategy:** Strategy which organizational decisions are determined by both analysis and unforeseen environmental developments.

## 2.2 STRATEGIC MANAGEMENT PROCESS

The strategic management process means defining the organization's strategy. It is also defined as the process by which managers make a choice of a set of strategies for the organization that will enable it to achieve better performance.

Strategic management is a continuous process that appraises the business and industries in which the organization is involved; appraises it's competitors; and fixes goals to meet all the present and future competitor's and then reassesses each strategy.

**Strategic management process has following four steps:**

- <u>Environmental Scanning</u>- Environmental scanning refers to a process of collecting, scrutinizing and providing information for strategic purposes. It helps in analyzing the internal and external factors influencing an organization. After executing the environmental analysis process, management should evaluate it on a continuous basis and strive to improve it.
- <u>Strategy Formulation</u>- Strategy formulation is the process of deciding best course of action for accomplishing organizational objectives and hence achieving organizational purpose. After conducting environment

scanning, managers formulate corporate, business and functional strategies.

- <u>Strategy Implementation</u>- Strategy implementation implies making the strategy work as intended or putting the organization's chosen strategy into action. Strategy implementation includes designing the organization's structure, distributing resources, developing decision making process, and managing human resources.
- <u>Strategy Evaluation</u>- Strategy evaluation is the final step of strategy management process. The key strategy evaluation activities are: appraising internal and external factors that are the root of present strategies, measuring performance, and taking remedial / corrective actions. Evaluation makes sure that the organizational strategy as well as it's implementation meets the organizational objectives.

These components are steps that are carried, in chronological order, when creating a new strategic management plan. Present businesses that have already created a strategic management plan will revert to these steps as per the situation's requirement, so as to make essential changes.

## 2.3 TOOLS AND TECHNIQUES OF STRATEGIC MANAGEMENT

There are several tools of strategic management, let us know discuss the most important and useful tools.

## I.  Porters 5 Forces

The Porter's Five Forces tool is a simple but powerful tool for understanding where power lies in a business situation. This is useful, because it helps you understand both the strength of your current competitive position, and the strength of a position you're considering moving into.

With a clear understanding of where power lies, you can take fair advantage of a situation of strength, improve a situation of weakness, and avoid taking wrong steps. This makes it an important part of your planning toolkit.

Conventionally, the tool is used to identify whether new products, services or businesses have the potential to be profitable. However it can be very illuminating when used to understand the balance of power in other situations.

**Understanding the Tool**

Five Forces Analysis assumes that there are five important forces that determine competitive power in a business situation. These are:

- **Supplier Power:** Here you assess how easy it is for suppliers to drive up prices. This is driven by the number of suppliers of each key input, the uniqueness of their product or service, their strength and control over you, the cost of switching from one to another, and so on. The fewer the supplier choices you have, and the more you need suppliers' help, the more powerful your suppliers are.

- **Buyer Power:** Here you ask yourself how easy it is for buyers to drive prices down. Again, this is driven by the number of buyers, the importance of each individual buyer to your business, the cost to them of switching from your products and services to those of someone else, and so on. If you deal with few, powerful buyers, then they are often able to dictate terms to you.

- **Competitive Rivalry:** What is important here is the number and capability of your competitors. If you have many competitors, and they offer equally attractive products and services, then you'll most likely have little power in the situation, because suppliers and buyers will go elsewhere if they don't get a good deal from you. On the other hand, if no-one else can do what you do, then you can often have tremendous strength.

- **Threat of Substitution:** This is affected by the ability of your customers to find a different way of doing what you do – for example, if you supply a unique software product that automates an important process, people may substitute by doing the process manually or by outsourcing it. If substitution is easy and substitution is viable, then this weakens your power.

- **Threat of New Entry:** Power is also affected by the ability of people to enter your market. If it costs little in time or money to enter your market and compete effectively, if there are few economies of scale in place, or if you have little protection for your key technologies, then new competitors can quickly enter your market and weaken your position. If you have strong and durable barriers to entry, then you can preserve a favorable position and take fair advantage of it.

**Example**

Martin Johnson is deciding whether to switch career and become a farmer – he's always loved the countryside, and wants to switch to a career where he's his own boss. He creates the following Five Forces Analysis as he thinks the situation through:

Porter's Five Forces Example: Buying a Farm

This worries him:

- The **threat of new entry** is quite high: if anyone looks as if they're making a sustained profit, new competitors can come into the industry easily, reducing profits.
- **Competitive rivalry** is extremely high: if someone raises prices, they'll be quickly undercut. Intense competition puts strong downward pressure on prices.
- **Buyer Power** is strong, again implying strong downward pressure on prices.
- There is some **threat of substitution.**
- Unless he is able to find some way of changing this situation, this looks like a very tough industry to survive in. Maybe he'll need to specialize in a sector of the market that's protected from some of these forces, or find a related business that's in a stronger position.

## II. Strategic Groups

A strategic group is defined as a group of corporations that employ the same or similar strategies in a particular industry. Hunt discovered that some companies follow very different strategies when compared with other companies in the same market and classified uniform industry sub-groups based on their value adding chain.

Those sub-groups, which display similar behaviour along key strategic dimensions, were called strategy groups. Porter discovered that individual strategic group members face similar threats and opportunities in the competitive market. Furthermore, similar resource configurations form protective barriers around the strategic groups.

The strategic behaviour and performance within a strategy group are very similar. The industry may consist of several or only one strategic group. A strategic group may consist of one or more members. (Müller-Stewens 2005)

In his book, Porter said a business's activities could be split into two categories: primary activities and support activities. Primary activities include the following:

- **Inbound logistics:** This refers to everything involved in receiving, storing and distributing the raw materials used in the production process.
- **Operations:** This is the stage where raw products are turned into the final product.
- **Outbound logistics:** This is the distribution of the final product to consumers.
- **Marketing and sales:** This stage involves activities like advertising, promotions, sales-force organization, selecting distribution channels, pricing, and managing customer relationships of the final product to ensure it is targeted to the correct consumer groups.
- **Service:** This refers to the activities that are needed to maintain the product's performance after it has been produced. This stage includes things like installation, training, maintenance, repair, warranty and after-sales services.

The support activities help the primary functions and comprise the following:

- **Procurement:** This is how the raw materials for the product are obtained.
- **Technology development:** Technology can be used across the board in the development of a product, including in the research and development stage, in how new products are developed and designed, and process automation.
- **Human resource management:** These are the activities involved in hiring and retaining the proper employees to help design, build and market the product.
- **Firm infrastructure:** This refers to an organization's structure and its management, planning, accounting, finance and quality-control mechanisms.

## III. SWOT and TOWS MATRIX

TOWS and SWOT are acronyms for different arrangements of the words Strengths, Weaknesses, Opportunities and Threats.

By analyzing the **external environment** (threats and opportunities), and your **internal environment** (weaknesses and strengths), you can use these techniques to think about the strategy of your whole organization, a department or a team. You can also use them to think about a process, a marketing campaign, or even your own skills and experience.

**Identifying Strategic Options**

SWOT or TOWS analysis helps you get a better understanding of the strategic choices that you face. (Remember that "strategy" is the art of determining how you'll "win" in business and life.) It helps you ask, and answer, the following questions: How do you:

- Make the most of your strengths?
- Circumvent your weaknesses?
- Capitalize on your opportunities?
- Manage your threats?

A next step of analysis, usually associated with the externally-focused TOWS Matrix, helps you think about the options that you could pursue. To do this you match external opportunities and threats with your internal strengths and weaknesses, as illustrated in the matrix below:

This helps you identify strategic alternatives that address the following additional questions:

- Strengths and Opportunities (SO) – How can you use your strengths to take advantage of the opportunities?
- Strengths and Threats (ST) – How can you take advantage of your strengths to avoid real and potential threats?
- Weaknesses and Opportunities (WO) – How can you use your opportunities to overcome the weaknesses you are experiencing?
- Weaknesses and Threats (WT) – How can you minimize your weaknesses and avoid threats?

**Using the Tool**

- Step 1: Print off our free <u>SWOT Worksheet</u> and perform a TOWS/ SWOT analysis, recording your findings in the space provided. This helps you understand what your strengths and weaknesses are, as well as identifying the opportunities and threats that you should be looking at.

- Step 2: Print off our free <u>TOWS Strategic Options Worksheet</u>, and copy the key conclusions from the SWOT Worksheet into the area provided (shaded in blue).
- Step 3: For each combination of internal and external environmental factors, consider how you can use them to create good strategic options:
- Strengths and Opportunities (SO) – How can you use your strengths to take advantage of these opportunities?
- Strengths and Threats (ST) – How can you take advantage of your strengths to avoid real and potential threats?
- Weaknesses and Opportunities (WO) – How can you use your opportunities to overcome the weaknesses you are experiencing?
- Weaknesses and Threats (WT) – How can you minimize your weaknesses and avoid threats?

## IV.  Boston Consulting Group (BCG) Matrix

BCG is a four celled matrix (a 2 * 2 matrix) developed by BCG, USA. It is the most renowned corporate portfolio analysis tool. It provides a graphic representation for an organization to examine different businesses in it's portfolio on the basis of their related market share and industry growth rates. It is a two dimensional analysis on management of SBU's (Strategic Business Units). In other words, it is a comparative analysis of business potential and the evaluation of environment.

According to this matrix, business could be classified as high or low according to their industry growth rate and relative market share.

Relative Market Share = SBU Sales this year leading competitors sales this year.

Market Growth Rate = Industry sales this year - Industry Sales last year.

The analysis requires that both measures be calculated for each SBU. The dimension of business strength, relative market share, will measure comparative advantage indicated by market dominance. The key theory underlying this is existence of an experience curve and that market share is achieved due to overall cost leadership.

BCG matrix has four cells, with the horizontal axis representing relative market share and the vertical axis denoting market growth rate. The mid-point of relative market share is set at 1.0. if all the SBU's are in same industry, the average growth rate of the industry is used. While, if all the SBU's are located in different industries, then the mid-point is set at the growth rate for the economy.

Resources are allocated to the business units according to their situation on the grid. The four cells of this matrix have been called as stars, cash cows, question marks and dogs. Each of these cells represents a particular type of business.

- **Stars**- Stars represent business units having large market share in a fast growing industry. They may generate cash but because of fast growing market, stars require huge investments to maintain their lead. Net cash flow is usually modest. SBU's located in this cell are attractive as they are located in a robust industry and these business units are highly competitive in the industry. If successful, a star will become a cash cow when the industry matures.
- **Cash Cows**- Cash Cows represents business units having a large market share in a mature, slow growing industry. Cash cows require little investment and generate cash that can be utilized for investment in other business units. These SBU's are the corporation's key source of cash, and are specifically the core business. They are the base of an organization. These businesses usually follow stability strategies. When cash cows loose their appeal and move towards deterioration, then a retrenchment policy may be pursued.
- **Question Marks**- Question marks represent business units having low relative market share and located in a high growth industry. They require huge amount of cash to maintain or gain market share. They require attention to determine if the venture can be viable. Question marks are generally new goods and services which have a good commercial prospective. There is no specific strategy which can be adopted. If the firm thinks it has dominant market share, then it can adopt expansion strategy, else retrenchment strategy can be adopted. Most businesses start as question marks as the company tries to enter a high growth market in which there is already a market-share. If ignored, then question marks may become dogs, while if huge investment is made, then they have potential of becoming stars.
- **Dogs**- Dogs represent businesses having weak market shares in low-growth markets. They neither generate cash nor require huge amount

of cash. Due to low market share, these business units face cost disadvantages. Generally retrenchment strategies are adopted because these firms can gain market share only at the expense of competitor's/rival firms. These business firms have weak market share because of high costs, poor quality, ineffective marketing, etc. Unless a dog has some other strategic aim, it should be liquidated if there is fewer prospects for it to gain market share. Number of dogs should be avoided and minimized in an organization.

## V.  Ansoff Matrix

The Ansoff Matrix was developed by H. Igor Ansoff and first published in the Harvard Business Review in 1957, in an article titled "<u>Strategies for Diversification</u>." It has given generations of marketers and business leaders a quick and simple way to think about the risks of growth.

Sometimes called the Product/Market Expansion Grid, the Matrix (see 1, below) shows four strategies you can use to grow. It also helps you analyze the risks associated with each one. The idea is that, each time you move into a new quadrant (horizontally or vertically), risk increases.

### 2.4 GENERIC STRATEGIES

Generic Competitive Strategy matrix was developed by Michel Porter. It tries to explain a firm's relative position within its industry determines whether a firm's profitability is above or below the industry average. The fundamental basis of above average profitability in the long run is sustainable competitive advantage. There are two basic types of competitive advantage a firm can possess: low cost or differentiation. The two basic types of competitive advantage combined with the scope of activities for which a firm seeks to achieve them, lead to three generic strategies for achieving above average performance in an industry: cost leadership, differentiation, and focus. The focus strategy has two variants, cost focus and differentiation focus.

I.  **Cost Leadership:** In cost leadership, a firm sets out to become the low cost producer in its industry. The sources of cost advantage are varied and depend on the structure of the industry. They may include the pursuit of economies of scale, proprietary technology, preferential access to raw materials and other factors. A low cost producer must find and exploit all sources of cost advantage. if a firm can achieve and sustain overall cost leadership, then it will be an above average performer in its industry, provided it can command prices at or near the industry average.

II. **Differentiation:** In a differentiation strategy a firm seeks to be unique in its industry along some dimensions that are widely valued by buyers. It selects one or more attributes that many buyers in an industry perceive as important, and uniquely positions itself to meet those needs. It is rewarded for its uniqueness with a premium price.

III. **Cost Focus:** Here a business seeks a lower-cost advantage in just on or a small number of market segments. The product will be basic - perhaps a similar product to the higher-priced and featured market leader, but acceptable to sufficient consumers. Such products are often called "me-too's". Examples of Cost Focus: Many smaller retailers featuring own-label or discounted label products.

IV. **Differentiation Focus:** In the differentiation focus strategy, a business aims to differentiate within just one or a small number of target market segments. The special customer needs of the segment mean that there are opportunities to provide products that are clearly different from competitors who may be targeting a broader group of customers. The important issue for any business adopting this strategy is to ensure that customers really do have different needs and wants - in other words that there is a valid basis for differentiation - and that existing competitor products are not meeting those needs and wants.

## 2.5 GRAND STRATEGIES

### I. Stability Strategy

When firms are satisfied with their current rate of growth and profit, they may decide to use a stability strategy. It is essentially continuation of existing strategies. This type of strategies is common in industry having relatively stable environment. Firms attempt to maintain their size, level of production & sales, serving almost the same customers group, performing same customers functions, produces with same technology and operate the current lines of business. These firms do not attempt to grow through sales or development of products or markets.

These strategies could be of two types:

1.  Maintaining of Status Quo: though zero percent of growth is not practically possible, small business firms desire satisfactory level of operation rather the growth.
2.  Sustainable Growth: Slow growth is desired rather than maintenance of status quo.

## II.  Growth Strategy

Firms try to grow by exploiting the opportunities in the environment. Organization may select growth strategy to increase their profit, sales, and market share.According to William Glueck "Growth strategy is one that an enterprise pursue when it increases its level of objective upwards, and a significant increment much higher than an exploration of past achievement level"

These strategies could be of four types:

1.  Concentric Expansion Strategy-The first route of growth is to expand the present line of business. It can be aim at market penetration, Market development and /or Product development
2.  Integration Strategy: Integration basically means combining activities relating to the present activity of a firm.Company performs number of activities to transform an input to output.Activities include right from procurement of raw materials to the production of finished goods.
3.  Expansion through Diversification: Is the process of entry into a business which is new to an organization either market wise or technology wise or both. Diversification may involve internal or external, related or unrelated, horizontal or vertical, either singly or collectively.
4.  Expansion through cooperation: This can be done through simultaneous competition and cooperation among firms for mutual benefit.

- Mergers: A merger is a combination of two or more organizations in which one acquires the assets and liabilities of the other in exchange for shares or cash, or both the organizations are dissolved, and the assets and liabilities are combined and new stock is issued.
- Takeovers ( Acquisions): : It is the attempt of one firm to acquire ownership or control over another firm against the wishes of the latter's management. One company takes over the other company.

- Joint ventures: Joint ventures occur when two or more companies join together to form a separate legal entity, where each of the partners own equal or near equal stake.
- :Strategic Alliances: In strategic Alliance, two or more partner join hands together for certain specified objectives, generally, for certain specific period. When this objectives are achieved, partners terminate their alliance.

## III.  Retrenchment strategies

Involves a reduction in the scope of a corporation's activity which also generally necessitates a reduction in number of employees, sales of assets associated with discontinued products, restructuring of debts and liquidations of firms.

These strategies could be three types

1. Turnaround Strategy: If the firm chooses to focus on way and means to reverse the process of decline, it adopts Turnaround strategy
2. Divestment Strategy: It involves the sale or liquidation of a portion of business, or major division, profit centre or SBU.
3. Liquidation Strategies: This involves closing down a firm and selling its assets. It is considered as a last resort because it leads to serious consequences such as loss of employment for workers and other employees, termination of opportunities where a firm could pursue any future activities, and stigma of failure.

## IV.  Portfolio Restructuring:

This strategy is combination of stability, growth, and retrenchment strategies. Combinations strategies may be involve implementations of two or more strategies simultaneously or sequentially.Firms may liquidate one unit, develop other unit, and allow the third unit to stabiles to improve the efficiency of the business and maximize the profitability.

This strategy is also called portfolio restructuring as it is a mix and percentage make up of the different types of business in the portfolio.

**CASE STUDY:PHILIP ELECTRONICS**

Philips Electronics is one of the world's biggest producers of medical equipment, consumer electronics, semi-conductors, flat screen technologies, and home appliances. A European company with a very product tradition of innovation, Philips has consistently led the world in developing many important technologies. For example, it helped pioneer medical X-ray technology, the audio-cassette, the electric shaver, and today current compact discs technology. Yet for all its creative flair in the labs, Philips has struggled to compete with the likes of Matsushita, Sony and Samsung in the marketplace.

A big factor behind Philip' outstanding record of innovation is that the company has long encouraged scientific research and big projects that yield potentially big payoffs. While cultivating innovations, Philips has traditionally marketed its products in different parts of the world separately. Although Philips originated in the Netherlands, the company has historically looked to larger markets in the US, Latin America, Asia and the rest of Europe for much of its growth. Philips was one of the first companies to formulate and implement a worldwide strategy that witnessed the steady growth and profitability of local operations. Many of Philips innovations over time came from large labs located throughout the US, Europe, Australia and Canada. Over time, Philips relied heavily on its regional affiliated to manufacture many of its leading-edge products for sale in national and more local markets.

The innovation driven strategy worked for Philips for many decades. Japanese rivals such as Matsushita Electric, Sony, JVC, and Toshiba began producing consumer electronics and other high technology products at lower unit costs. Unlike Philips, Japanese firms were able to construct large factories that were ultra efficient. They were able to overtake Philips' market position in many markets. Philips also faced competition, and difficulties building up a well-recognized brand name with global reach.

Philips attempted to restructure its operations to compete more effectively with these rivals over the past two decades. Its current CEO Gerard Kleisterlee is overseeing a major reorganizations of Philips that seeks to combine disparate operations and organizational practices into a cohesive system. Kleisterlee wants Phillips traditionally separate business units to communicate and to coordinate their activities to achieve significant cost savings and to deliver leading edge products to market faster. At the same time, the company has decided to allocate more resources to high growth opportunities in its core medical, electronics, and flat screen business.

In addition, Philips has formed a wide array of technologies sharing relation ships with companies throughout the US and Far East. With LG group Philips formed a separate company known as LG Philips of LCD screens that are found in flat screen TVs and Cell phones and digital cameras. Philips teamed with Chinese maker of medical equipment known as Neusoft, will produce medical imaging equipment for use in china. In the filed of advanced integrated circuits, Philips joined with Taiwan Semiconductor company to co design and co-produce leading edge chips that will power next generation applicants and consumer electronics. It is also working with Samsung Electronic to create "electronic wallet", it has also an ambition to be an important supplier of new digital technologies for future home entertainment centers.

Philips strategic transition is designed to compete more effectively in an increasingly connected global marketplace. However the process of chaining Philips organizational practices represents a long term ongoing effort that has already helped the company become more profitable and faster moving.

# CHAPTER THREE

# ADVERTISING FOR ENTREPRENEURS

**3.1 INTRODUCTION TO ADVERTISING**

Advertising provides a direct line of communication to your existing and prospective customers about your product or service.

The purpose of advertising is to:

I. Make customers aware of your product or service;
II. Convince customers that your company's product or service is right for their needs;
III. Create a desire for your product or service;
IV. Enhance the image of your company;
V. Announce new products or services;
VI. Reinforce salespeople's messages;
VII. Make customers take the next step (ask for more information, request a sample, place an order, and so on); and
VIII. Draw customers to your business.

Your advertising goals should be established in your business plan. For example, you may want to obtain a certain percentage of growth in sales, generate more inquiries for sales, or build in-store traffic. The desired result can simply be increasing name recognition or modifying the image you're projecting. Objectives vary depending on the industry and market you're in.

All products and businesses go through three stages, with different advertising goals for each one.

1. **The start-up business.** You're new in the market and need to establish your identity. Your company needs high levels of promotion and publicity to grab consumers' attention.

2. **The growing business.** Once your identity is established, you need to differentiate yourself from your competition and convince buyers that yours is the service or product to try.

3. **The established business.** The purpose at this point is to remind consumers why they should continue buying from you.

No matter which stage your business is in, advertising follows four steps, according to the industry mnemonic, "AIDA: Awareness, Interest, Desire, Action." Your job is to make prospective customers aware that your product or service exists, pique their interest in what your product or service can do for them, make them want to try your product or service, and finally take action, by asking for more information or actually buying the product.

**3.2 ADVERTISING CAMPAIGN**

When developing an advertising campaign, complete the following four-step procedure:

- Define your market. Determine who your target market is (those customers most likely to buy your product or service). One magazine that's fun to read, interesting and helpful in this regard is American Demographics.
- Establish your budget. Know what you can afford to spend to reach your target audience.
- Plan which media you'll use. out what are the best ways to reach your prospective customers with your message.
- Create an advertising strategy. Choose the most effective message and visuals for your advertising campaign.

**Process**

1. **Research:** first step is to do a market research for the product to be advertised. One needs to find out the product demand, competitors, etc.
2. **Know the target audience:** one need to know who are going to buy the product and who should be targeted.
3. **Setting the budget:** the next step is to set the budget keeping in mind all the factors like media, presentations, paper works, etc which have a role in the process of advertising and the places where there is a need of funds.

4. **Deciding a proper theme:** the theme for the campaign has to be decided as in the colors to be used, the graphics should be similar or almost similar in all ads, the music and the voices to be used, the designing of the ads, the way the message will be delivered, the language to be used, jingles, etc.

5. **Selection of media:** the media or number of Medias selected should be the one which will reach the target customers.

6. **Media scheduling:** the scheduling has to be done accurately so that the ad will be visible or be read or be audible to the targeted customers at the right time.

### 3.3 TYPES OF ADVERTISING

Advertising has evolved into a vastly complex form of communication, with literally thousands of different ways for a business to get a message to the consumer. Today's advertiser has a vast array of choices at his or her disposal. The Internet alone provides many of these, with the advent of branded viral videos, banners, advertorials, sponsored websites, branded chat rooms and so much more.

1. <u>Online Advertising (aka Digital)</u>

If you see an advertisement via the Internet (World Wide Web), then it is classified <u>as online advertising</u>. In fact, there are ads on this very page, and most other websites you visit, as they are the primary revenue driver for the Internet. Another avenue of online advertising is "Native Advertising," which is the digital variation of the old print advertorials. And, sponsored content is growing by leaps and bounds. From ads on Facebook and SnapChat, to partnerships with Buzzfeed and Reddit, the fastest, easiest way to reach millions of potential customers is online.

1. <u>Cell Phone & Mobile Advertising</u>

A relatively new form of advertising compared to the others, but one that's dominating the media mix, uses <u>cell phones</u>, iPads, Kindles, Nooks, and other portable electronic devices with Internet connectivity. Current trends in mobile advertising involve major use of social media such as Twitter, Instagram, Snapchat, and Facebook.Right now, this is the toughest nut to crack. This kind of advertising is not only disruptive, but can leave the customers with a lot of ill will. If you do it, do it right. For a while, native advertising was a good way to get into the feed, but even that has come under scrutiny for being deceptive.

3.  Print Advertising

Once a huge driver of sales, print is taking a back seat to the many digital forms of advertising now available to marketers. However, if there is one thing that's certain about advertising, it's that being different is good. And when consumers tire of digital ads, a return to printed pieces, and the tactile feeling and permanence they provide, is definitely on the cards. Typically, print can be split into three sub-categories:

4.  **Periodical Advertising**

If it's in a magazine, a newspaper, or anything else that comes out at regular intervals, then it's periodical advertising (aka a print ad). For decades, print ads were the gold standard for advertisers and their clients. To grab the center spread of a big magazine, or the back cover of a newspaper, meant millions of people were seeing the message.

5.  **Brochures, Leaflets, Flyers, Handouts and Point of Sale Advertising**

Although some of these can be placed within the pages of newspapers and magazines, they are treated as a separate entity (usually because they have less chance of being seen). From something that sits on a counter or customer service desk, to a glossy car brochure, this is a more intimate, and long-form, way of engaging the consumer. Use this when you have more information than you can cram into a print ad.

6.  **Direct MailAdvertising**

Either of the techniques mentioned above can be incorporated into direct mail. It simply means that your printed pieces are mailed direct to the consumer. This is a technique that has been, and continues to be, abused by inferior marketing agencies that have turned the craft into "junk mail." Done right, direct mail can be a fantastic way to engage the customer, if it is creative and intelligently conceived and executed. Do not count it out.

### 7.  Guerrilla Advertising

Also known as ambient media, guerrilla advertising (or marketing) has become prominent over the last 20 years. It is a broadly used term for anything unconventional, and usually invites the consumer to participate or interact with the piece in some way. Location is important, as is timing. The driving forces behind guerrilla advertising or marketing are creative ideas and innovation, not a large budget.

Quite often, you will ask for forgiveness rather than permission with these campaigns, and they will spread via word of mouth and social media.

### 8.  Broadcast Advertising

A mass-market form of communication including television and radio, broadcast advertising has, until recently, been the most dominant way to reach a large number of consumers. Broadcast advertising has really taken a beating over the last few years, especially with the rise of DVRs and "ad skipping" technology. However, it is still a popular way to reach millions of people, especially when the Super Bowl comes around.

### 9.  Outdoor Advertising

Also known as out-of-home (OOH) advertising, this is a broad term that describes any type of advertising that reaches the consumer when he or she is outside of the home. You will know it as billboards, bus shelter posters, fly posters, and even those big digital boards in Times Square.

### 10.  Public Service Advertising

Unlike traditional commercials, Public Service Advertisements (PSA) are primarily designed to inform and educate rather than sell a product or service. PSAs traditionally appear on TV and radio, but are also being heavily promoted online these days.

### 11.  Product Placement Advertising

In a nutshell, product placement is the promotion of branded goods and services within the context of a show or movie, rather than as an explicit advertisement. If you have ever seen a movie and wondered "wow, they sure are driving a lot of Ford cars in this scene," or "does everyone in this TV show drink Pepsi?" then you are noticing product placement. It's a way that these films and shows get funding, and is a great way for advertisers to reach a targeted demographics

## CASE STUDY

### KEYS FOR A SUCCESSFUL BANNER ADCAMPAIGN

Here are the 3 important key points you should check when you are about to make your banner ad campaign:

1. PLACEMENT

Everybody is talking about banner blindness but if you look closer at what the users tell you "with their eyes" you will find new ways to display your banners in the place where the user will click on them.

So, if you want to make your website gain more leads, I recommend you to start using some eye tracking apps. I truly recommend you apps like CrazyEgg or SumoMe.

Sometimes, the placement "above the fold" does offer the best visibility, but engagement is not always about location.

The solution is to find unusual placements that do not interrupt the content experience but gain attention and drive higher engagement.

2. RELEVANCE

Start with 2 things on your mind when you think that this ad will be the one that makes the user click on it:

Is this relevant for this audience?

How relevant is this for the audience?

Because consumers are more likely to click and engage with an ad that provides relevant service – informing them about a product they are looking for, taking them to a landing page or website for more information on a subject they are interested in.

But the most important thing is that users don't want to be interrupted with an irrelevant ad.

So think about this, do you want to gain a negative attention from the user that will click on the "x" sign on your banner ad or do you want a positive attention were the user will engage with your brand?

3. EXPERIENCE

You can find in this report that unconventionally placed ads break banner blindness and drive engagement. And another important fact is to understand how the ad unit was designed with the user experience in mind.

Why they were designed to enhance content, not to disrupt it and why they were created to engage rather than dismiss.

So make sure that your banner ads helps the user on your website have a great experience at the right moment, in the right place for the right person.

# CHAPTER FOUR

# CHANGE LEADERSHIP

## 4.1 CHANGE

"Effective change leadership happens when leaders of change provide direction, guidance and support to the people who are implementing the change as well as those having to adapt to change."

**Causes for change**

**<u>The 3 key phases of change leadership</u>**

Harking back to Kurt Levin's original change model of unfreeze, change, refreeze, its useful to consider the implications of change leadership in the current situation, the transition and the future state.

The key aspect of this is how the role and behavior of change leaders has to adapt over time. As change leaders move from one side of this process to the other their role evolves. Initially they help kick-start the change through challenging the status quo and expressing their dissatisfaction with the current situation. Next they show support for the transition via both private and public demonstrations. Finally these leaders reinforce the future state and take a strong stance on activities like effectively role modelling the change.

## 4.2 BUILDING EFFECTIVE CHANGE LEADERSHIP IN YOUR ORGANIZATION

Despite a wealth of literature dedicated to considering whether effective leaders – and by implication change leaders – are born or can be nurtured, we think that the process of developing change leadership is something that any company can work on.

In any change management programme, there's a clear process with a number of steps that organisations can work through to enhance leadership as follows

1. *Map out a change network*

When people talk about change leadership, they are often only thinking about the executive level, when in fact change leadership exists at multiple levels throughout the organisation. The initial drive might come from the top, but in order to sustain change you need the impact of a whole network of individuals throughout the organisation, including local managers. In fact, when change projects fail to sustain, it's often local managers who are the sticking point. Looking at a standard organisational chart won't tell you what this change network looks like. Mapping the change network is a formal process of identifying key players in a change initiative, clarifying the relationships between them and assigning them roles such as sponsor, influencer and change agent.

### 1. *Engage sponsors at every level*

Received wisdom has taught us that enlisting the support of an executive project sponsor at a very senior level is key to the success of a major change. But while the executive sponsor is the single point of accountability and the person who makes the big decisions, in reality a change project will also have a number of local sponsors and their role should not be underestimated.

Sponsors fulfil a number of functions in the change process including:

- **Accountability**-They are ultimately responsible for making a success of the project.
- **Authority**- They lend their weight to the change, supporting people who are adapting to the change and managing any resistance.
- **Decision making**-They make the key decisions and support change agents over smaller decisions.
- **Support**-By lending their support; they legitimize the change initiative at every level of the organisation.

### 3. *Develop informal influencers*

In an age of social networking and viral media, we are only too aware of the influence of informal communications. In fact, the subconscious nudge, as demonstrated in Richard Thaler and Cass Sunstein's book 2 , can be more powerful and effective as an influencer than formal authorities telling people to change.

In an organisational context, it's important to ensure key people are supporting a change project, particularly at an early stage when executive support may not be as fully formed as you might like it to be. It's really a case of recognising who the informal influencers are through the change network mapping exercise, then bringing them onside before they have had a chance to form an adverse opinion.

Informal influencers fall into four main categories:

- **Advocates**, who persuade other people that change is a good idea.
- **Connectors**, who can help connect to others who you may not have a relationship with.
- **Controllers**, who control access to information or people.
- **Experts**, with technical expertise

4. *Arm change agents with the right skills for the job*

Change agents are the day-to-day instigators of change and they support the sponsor's intentions. They fulfill a number of roles, from planning and executing project plans to helping overcome resistance and building momentum towards the desired future state. There are two sides to the instruction of change agents. Firstly, organisations need to ensure they pick the best people for the job in hand. Secondly, change agents need the right skills for the job. If there are gaps in their skills base, these should be plugged through training or coaching.

These include:

- A good understanding of change principles Skills in collecting and using data
- Knowledge of running meetings and workshops
- Good planning and project management skills
- Communications expertise
- The ability to manage resistance and deal with uncertainty

5. *Embrace change*

Change programmes typically follow one of four approaches, each of which corresponds to a different leadership style. Let's initially consider the first three approaches here.

- **Technical:** breaking the change down into a series of functional tasks and outcomes. Leaders tend to be autocratic, aggressively forcing through change while ignoring employee concerns. They build short-term gains, but their approach can lead to pitfalls and long-term resentment.

- **Emotional:** appealing to the hearts and minds of the workforce, without necessarily creating a proper structure to the initiative. Visionary leaders will pre-announce an initiative without consulting local managers who will be affected by the change and without necessarily thinking through the consequences. On the other side, sympathetic leaders pay too much attention to how people feel about the change, rather than leading them through it.

- **Bolt-on:** where change agents are expected to see through a change on top of their regular job. A recent survey by the Society for Human Resource Management found that while organisations experience on average 2.1 changes per year, 77% of HR departments did not have the resources to manage change3 . In this approach leaders may put financial incentives in place to reward adoption of the change, but they don't have enough time to think through the real consequences and fail to role model and get involved in change because they are too busy doing their regular jobs.

### 4.3 KOTTERS 8 STEPS FOR LEADING CHANGE

Dr. John Kotter studied the progress of over 100 companies during the change situation.In 1995, Prof.Dr.John Kotter introduced 8 steps for leading change in his book called " leading Change'

It is an appropriate organizational development tool, providing a three dimensional linkage between individuals, groups and the organization. Thus, this model causes change to become a campaign for the change management.

**Step 1: Increase Urgency**

- Plan and take a action to initiate for the required changes, the actions should be motivating and booming.

- The state of the organization should be determined before conducting this phase as
- Complacency
- False urgency
- True urgency

- Strategy that should be adopted are as follows:

- Explaining and realizing the benefit of change.
- Creating and developing opportunities for the users
- Clear communication and information procedure.
- Convincing the major supporting groups and motivating them
- Value creating and inspiring proposal for the change.

**Step 2: Build guiding teams**

- Guiding teams must be formed so that the activities such as Developing vision, communication and so on can be performed.
- Effective team must be constructed and trust should be developed between the team members.
- **Strategies that should be followed are:**
- The team as a whole should reflect enough power so that those left out cannot block progress.
- All relevant viewpoints should be represented so that informed intelligent decisions can be made with strong trust and commitment.
- The group should be seen and respected by those in the firm so that the group can enhance their credibility.
- Recognize the opportunities and build the capacity of leading the change.

**Step 3: create a change Vision**

- Gives an appropriate feel of understanding the reason for the change.
- Vision must be focused, flexible and easy to communicate.

- Strategies to develop the vision are:

- They convey a clear picture of what the future will look like and should be imaginable.
- Stakeholders should show interest with high desirability
- The goal should be realistic and attainable for the vision.
- It should be focused.
- Vision should be flexible.
- They should be easy to communicate and can be explained quickly.

### Step 4: communication for buying

- The developed vision as it is updated must be communicated among the members.
- **Strategies for the communication of the vision are:**
- Communication should be done simple and formal language.
- It should be vivid using verbal pictures which is more worthy than a thousand words-use metaphor, analogy, and example.
- Ideas should be able to spread to all the persons.
- Two way communication is always more powerful than one way communication.

### Step 5 : Enable actions

- In this step, the guiding teams turns their attention in the mitigation of the obstacles that do not support the change vision.
- It also involves the investment in the employee for their managerial training and development.
- **Strategies for empowering change action are given below:**
- Hire change leaders to deliver results on vision.
- Gain consistent feed back
- Immediate action to remove obstacles that block the change.

### Step 6 : Create short term wins

- A short term win can be defined as an effective organizational improvement that can be achieved within 6 to 18 months.
- A short term win must follow following criteria:
- Its success must be unambiguous.
- It should be visible throughout the organization.

- It should be related with the change effort.

**Step 7: Build on the change**

- The senior leadership must keep the urgency level high to effect the change using the organizational power and the lower level managers must work with the guiding coalition to identify and remove the unnecessary dependencies and bring the change project to the possible as it is expected.

**Step 8: anchor the changes in corporate culture**

- Conduct a discussion program with employees.
- Explain the importance of change ideals and values when hiring the people and conducting trainings
- Develop new policies and processes that reinforce the value of change.

# 4.4 HIGHLY EFFECTIVE CHANGE LEADERS

In today's rapidly changing business environment, quickly identifying new opportunities and taking action to capture them is no longer the private domain of industry leaders—it is a matter of survival for every business and for every employee. As Pulitzer prize-winning author Thomas Friedman noted in his book,*The World is Flat*, not just every company, but every individual is competing today in a global economy.

Today's landscape is a Darwinian world. The winners and losers of this global competition are determined by one factor: change. Today's competitors are moving so fast, that products and jobs get quickly commoditized or even eliminated. Those individuals and companies that identify new opportunities and take the necessary actions to capture them will survive. Those who learn to do it over and over will thrive. In other words, companies and individuals must learn how to change and treat change leadership as a mission-critical discipline.

It is worth noting that learning how to learn, learning how to innovate, and learning how to change are all closely related. The notion of "change" is arguably the most powerful because it focuses on results and implies proactive movement from one place to another. For example, if you ask your employee, "What did you learn today?" it begs the question, "What did you do differently afterward?", which begs the next question, "And what was the result?". Contrast that with asking your employee, "What did you change today?" The question implies continuous improvement. It manifests the notion that doing what you did yesterday, being as good as you were yesterday, is not acceptable. Imagine if each of your employees changed one thing every day. That's approximately 240 improvements per employee per year. What would that do for your business?

While being a change leader may not be easy, the first step is knowing what it requires. People who are effective leaders of change have six characteristics. As a supervisor and leader, knowing these six characteristics helps you in several ways. First, you want to cultivate these qualities in yourself. Second, you can factor these characteristics into your hiring decisions. Third, you will want to cultivate these characteristics in your team culture by taking steps to reinforce them and avoiding steps that contradict them. Here are the six characteristics of change leaders:

**1) Low Level of Anxiety**

Anxieties are emotions and beliefs that prevent us from coping effectively with our current circumstances. Anxieties stem mostly from past negative experiences that continue to generate strong negative emotions. For example, many children who grew up in poverty during the Great Depression continued to live in fear of poverty, literally saving pennies in glass jars, despite achieving economic success in adulthood. But, current circumstances can also be the source of fear, uncertainly, and doubt. For example, employee reward systems that pit colleagues against one another in gladiator-like competitions that reward winners and penalize losers may cause employees to constantly look over their shoulder to see who is going to stab them in the back next.

Anxieties wield enormous influence on our behavior, usually resulting in one of two responses. People usually either a) erect strong defenses, figuratively digging fox holes to protect themselves, or b) go on the attack, making sure to harm and disable the perceived threat, before it can hurt them. These are destructive behaviors that not only prevent people from responding effectively to change, but can also harm others around them. To perform at the highest level and to drive innovation and change, people must have a sense of security and be unencumbered by anxieties.

*Supervisor's Tip:* Hire people with low levels of anxiety and create an environment where people feel secure, rather than threatened.

## 2) Emotional Stability

To learn well and perform at a high level, people must be in a good mood. One of the definitions of the word mood is, "a frame of mind disposed or receptive, as to some activity or thing." Large swings from levels of depression to elation and back to depression do not put people in a mental state that is receptive and ready for constructive action. One landmine to avoid is "breaking" an employee's attitude and belief that s/he can succeed in the job. Once an employee crosses a certain line toward depression, they become locked in a vicious cycle where their performance suffers, which causes further depression, which further reduces their performance, and so on. At that point, you've lost the employee.

*Supervisor's Tip:* Hire people whose emotional wiring is permanently connected to "happy" and take daily action to maintain a high level of enthusiasm among your team.

## 3) Action Orientation

Adapting to and leading change requires action. Being receptive to learning is not sufficient. The purpose of learning is to then take action and achieve the goal. People who have low levels of energy and are inclined to sit and watch will be the last to learn and adapt to change. Effective leaders are inclined to step up and participate in the action. They feel energized and exhilarated by the action and the progress.

*Supervisor's Tip:* Hire people with high energy levels and have events and activities that stimulate action and energy. Note: This requires that you allow time for these activities. Don't tell people there is a 3PM team volleyball game and also give them a 4PM deadline for a project.

## 4) Confidence

By definition, learning, innovating, and changing require exploration of the unknown. It is natural to feel anxious about stepping into unknown territory. Exploration is not without risks. Scurvy, cannibals, poisonous snakes, avalanches, new suppliers that fail to deliver—the hazards that have befallen explorers are innumerable. But, new opportunities can only be identified by exploring the unknown. Therefore, people must hold the belief that, despite the unknown risks, the unknown outcomes will be positive. In other words, they must be confident in their ability to succeed.

*Supervisor's Tip:* Hire people who are not afraid to take risks and have experienced the sweet taste of success in the past. Also, consider measuring and rewarding the exploration process itself, rather than worshiping the "conquistadors" who have blazed new trails. True innovation requires knocking on many doors before finding the one that opens. So, it is important to maintain an appropriate perspective.

### 5) Openness

To explore new ideas and learn how to apply them one must be receptive to them. We can always think of a million reasons something won't work. But, if we open our minds to the possibilities, we can also find many ways new ideas can work. But, simply being receptive is not enough, Harvard psychologist Ellen Langer says we must be "mindful". By mindful she means being constantly attentive and exposing our minds to many different perspectives. We are able to see more ways new ideas can work if we equip ourselves with a vast repertoire of perspectives and ideas.

*Supervisor's Tip:* Hire people who have diverse experiences and multidimensional skills. Give employees "white space" between the normal duties in their job description and encourage them to gain different experiences and perspectives.

### 6) Risk Tolerance

At first glance high risk tolerance may seem synonymous with high confidence. The difference is that confidence is an attitude and a belief that is accepted on faith, while risk is a mathematical concept that can be measured and managed. All actions involve risk and uncertainty—including the "action" of staying in the same place. In fact the world is changing so fast, that staying in the current position could be the riskiest proposition of all—like standing in the middle of a highway. But, dealing with risk doesn't mean simply rolling the dice and accepting your fate. A healthy risk tolerance means taking all possible steps to mitigate or eliminate risks, and then making a well-calculated, highly likely bet.

*Supervisor's Tip:* Rather than penalizing your staff when they fail, encourage them to take risk. Furthermore, rather than measuring outcomes, which is a "no-brainer", be a value-added supervisor by measuring and coaching your staff on how well they manage risk.

In conclusion, if you use the six characteristics of change leaders as hiring criteria, then build those characteristics into the culture of your organization, your team will discover and exploit new opportunities that will put you ahead of your competition.

### 4.5 RISK MANAGEMENT

Risk management is the identification, assessment, and prioritization of <u>risks</u> followed by coordinated and economical application of resources to minimize, monitor, and control the probability and/or impact of unfortunate events or to maximize the realization of opportunities.

Risk management's objective is to assure <u>uncertainty</u> does not deflect the endeavor from the business goals

## Principles of risk management

Risk management should:

- create <u>value</u> – resources expended to mitigate risk should be less than the consequence of inaction, or (as in <u>value engineering</u>), the gain should exceed the pain
- be an integral part of organizational processes
- be part of decision making process
- explicitly address uncertainty and assumptions
- be a systematic and structured process
- be based on the best available information
- be tailorable
- take human factors into account
- be transparent and inclusive
- be dynamic, iterative and responsive to change
- be capable of continual improvement and enhancement
- be continually or periodically re-assessed

## The Role of leadership in Risk management

This observation is one of the thousands shared by the 300 C-suite executives, who participated in a series of candid discussions spearheaded by a group of Ivey faculty over the past year. Our basic purpose in bringing together these executives was to find out if better leadership could have made a difference in preventing the financial meltdown that led to the recent global economic crisis.

We found out that good leadership could have and certainly did make a difference, especially with respect to risk management. Many of the business and public sector organizations which emerged unscathed from the meltdown did see the dangers looming on the horizon. It was apparent that their people understood the potential impact and wider implications of these problems and took immediate steps to circumvent them. Essentially, these organizations had cultures attuned to potential risks with the ability to manage the dynamics effectively.

By contrast, those who suffered the most during the crisis did not seem to anticipate the risks or problems ahead, especially those that could reverberate across markets and borders. For instance, when people speak about the banks, brokerage firms and investment companies which fared so poorly during the crisis, some of the biggest questions revolve around risk. How could they not have known the risks? And if they did know, why didn't they do something sooner? Were they too timid to tackle the problems, hoping they would just go away? Why didn't they understand the ramifications of their actions? Could they not foresee how their decisions would inevitably ripple across companies and countries to affect others? Did they even care that investors could lose money?

Based on my experience, as a former CEO and as educator of business leaders, the executives leading these organizations should have known about the risks. They should have acted and acted quickly. And they should have felt compelled to act, basically because it was both the right and the smart thing to do. As the business leader from Montreal quoted above believes, policies and procedures are not enough. It is the leader's responsibility to manage risk effectively.

How do business leaders achieve effective risk management? Fundamentally, I believe they do three simple things well. First, they ask the right questions. Clearly, some very complicated investment products were developed at the height of this bubble. Many executives and board directors admitted that they did not understand the mathematics or the economics behind many of these products. But as we found during our research, the effective leaders probed the experts about how these products were designed. Consequently, they learned that the underlying assumptions supporting these products were wrong. Or if they did not understand them, they chose not to offer them.

For other leaders, asking the right or the difficult questions was just too much work. They did not want to rock the boat, especially when market was going up and up. These leaders neglected the often difficult and uncomfortable role of a leader. Sometimes you have to shake up the status quo. As our research revealed, the leaders who did ask the hard questions discovered soon enough that if something seems too good to be true, it usually is.

Second, the best leaders consult with a mix of people, with different perspectives, backgrounds and knowledge to predict, assess and manage risk. They consult with others not only within their own immediate spheres of influence but in other industries and sectors. By contrast, some of the firms that fared so badly during the crisis seemed to breed exclusive clubs for like-minded people. The people in these isolated groups were getting very rich, very fast. They got caught up in the success of the moment. Worse still, they believed they would never lose. They also came to believe that they were much smarter than everyone else, both inside and outside their firms. Consequently, they did not listen to people who brought different points of view to the discussion.

Unfortunately, the leaders in these companies perpetuated this thinking, setting the wrong example for everyone else in the firm. Employees with a contrarian thought, new evidence or a question that disputed the contentions of the "club", soon learned to shut up and put up. As a result, there was no critical testing of ideas or assumptions and their potential consequences.

This very same situation arose at the height of the telecom bubble. Some people recognized that there was a bandwidth glut. They realized that some companies were developing products and services for a market that didn't exist. But in the midst of absurdly high corporate valuations, some leaders and their people chose to ignore the facts.

By contrast, good leaders welcome different opinions and points of views. Because of this, they are aware of potential risks and have the ability to make more informed and inevitably wiser decisions. Our research about the global financial meltdown showed that receptiveness to diverse viewpoints and opinions often defined the cultures of companies that survived the crisis and continue to thrive.

Third, the most effective leaders during the global financial meltdown were people of good character. They had integrity, courage and compassion. They were careful, prudent and aware of their limitations. As such, they were sensitive about the risks of harming their shareholders through shaky investments. They made sure that any decision they made or any action taken by their firms would ultimately be good for their companies, their shareholders and their customers. Overall, they exhibited an unrelenting determination to contribute to the good of the organization they serve, the people who follow them and the communities in which they operate.

By contrast, the worst failing exhibited by some leaders before, during and after the crisis, is that they just did not care about what might happen to other people. Some knew that their companies were building a deck of cards destined to collapse. They must have realized that people could get hurt, and that some investors could lose their life savings. Nevertheless, it didn't seem to matter.

In summary, policies and procedures for predicting, evaluating and managing risk are important. But if leaders don't ask the right questions, if they don't seek out a diversity of opinions and perspectives, and if they don't act with integrity, these rules won't make any difference. And when that happens, the blame for the damaging consequences rests solely with leadership.

**CASE STUDY**
**<u>SHAKING OFF THE STIGMA</u>**

The biggest challenge Brand Modi faced was diverting public attention away from the 2002 communal riots in Gujarat that claimed the lives of more than 1,000 people, mostly Muslims. Initially, Modi's supporters in BJP attempted to engage in public debate and highlight the clean chit given by courts to wash off the stigma. Then, they changed tack. They toned down the Hindutva rheotoric and focused instead on Modi's more recent past and his development record in Gujarat. "He knows that people want a better life and he offers Hindutva with the right dilution," says Desai of Future Brands.

Marketing gurus cite the examples of Cadbury, PepsiCo and Coca-Cola that battled problems relating to brand-taint. Cadbury had fought its way out of a controversy related to worms in its chocolates while the two beverages giants faced allegations of pesticides in their colas. "The best way for a tainted brand to overcome a challenge is to not talk too much, but to acknowledge it happened, and then move on," says Samu, the ISB professor. "The more one talks about, the more the memory for that event gets activated among the target market, and they remember it more. The BJP and Modi did not talk about it. Or if they did, they kept it to a minimum," he adds.

IIM-Bangalore's Moorthi says the weakness of the Congress leadership also helped boost Brand Modi. "When the brands in the domain appear worse, the contending brand might shine by comparison. In Modi's case, he was helped by the tightlipped nature of the Congress leadership and their indifferent performance in the second stint," he says.

While most companies routinely apologize for problems detected in their products, Modi stopped short of doing so. "He did give an account of reflections on the event [the riots]. He seemed to say that he was pained about the event but didn't say sorry," says Moorthi. Veteran adman Prahlad Kakkar concurs. "It does not matter if he [Modi] is wrong. He will never publicly admit that," observes Kakkar, who has been associated with several political campaigns, including that of Indira Gandhi. "But he will, at the same time, take corrective measures to navigate out of it, without ever saying so."

# CHAPTER FIVE

# SUCESSION PLANNING

## 5.1 SUCESSION PLANNING

The absence of a succession plan can seriously hamper the growth prospects of an organisation. Imagine disastrous consequences when there is a sudden vacuum at the top level. There is no one to steer the Critical plans needing immediate action get postponed. The organisation remains headless and directionless a while. Suitable candidates may not be available internally, as no one has been groomed in the past, keeping such an eventuality in mind. Bringing in outsiders may mitigate the crisis temporarily but the long-term impact is bound to be negative. Internal forces may start a rebellion and create tug-of-war situations frustrating regularity. (Wallum)

Succession planning is, "The process of ensuring a suitable supply of successors for current and future senio key jobs arising from business strategy, so that the careers of individuals can be planned and managed optimise the organisations' needs and the individuals' aspirations."

The purpose of succession planning is to identify and develop people to replace current jobholders in position-so Through succession planning, companies assure a steady flow of internal talent to fill important vacancies. Succession planning encourages 'hiring from within' and creates a healthy environment where employees have careers and not merely jobs. It helps in identifying human resource shortages and skill shortages before openings occur. Thereafter, it becomes easy to groom qualified candidates for future vacancies. The organization is, thus, assured of continuity of operations and better-qualified incumbents. Preparing a schedule for succession is critical to success of the company,especially at the top level.When the baton changes over a period of time,disruption and dislocation is minimized.Indeed,when a new CEO is meant to consolidate on the past successes,slow shift is ideal. If qualified candidates are not available within the company,outsiders can be considered readily for the possible openings.Complete dependence on succession from within or from outside is not desirable.Internal candidates require a pat on the back when they do well.External candidates are needed for injecting fresh blood into the company

### Replacement Charts

A succession plan is a plan for identifying who is currently in post and who is available and qualified to take over in the event of retirement, voluntary retirement, dismissal or sickness. A typical succession chart shows details of key executives and brief references to their possible successors

The replacement chart is a visual representation of who will replace whom if there is a job opening. The replacement summary indicates likely replacements for each job and shows their relative strengths and weaknesses. This can be prepared in a detailed way so as to facilitate the easy selection of a candidate in case of future vacancies.

### Career Planning vs Succession Planning

The terms 'career planning' and 'succession planning' are not synonymous, but they are similar. Succession planning is generally needed for key positions at higher levels, while career planning covers executives at all levels including high skilled employees and operatives. Career planning, by its very nature, includes succession planning. The career paths for executives are identified. How people can grow vertically is also indicated. In case of a vacancy arising at any level, the career plan is well supported by a succession chart. Both are thus complementary and interdependent.

### The Indian Scenario

Evidently, to have sustained growth, every company needs a succession plan. But most managers and owners exhibit a kind of aversion to nurture talent in advance for various reasons. Most Public Sector undertaking (PSUs) find it difficult to fill the top-level vacancies in time, due to political interference. Internal policies like cadre-based seniority (career progression can take place only within the respective cadre), approved manpower strength (a competent person maybe denied promotion only becaus~ all the approved posts in the next grade are full), union agreements (promotions are based on union agreements favouring seniority) and reservation quotas (for backward, economically weaker sections of society) have also complicated the process of picking up the right candidate at the right time. As a result, many PSUs, banks and financial institutions remained headless in the past for a painfully long time. (Nair; Singh and news items in Economic Times and Business Standard) Due to rebellion from internal groups, Air India had to bring in the ex-chairman of a steel company (of course without any success) to run the show. The situation is no better in the private sector. When Thermax's chief died suddenly, his wife Anu Aga had to step in . without any previous experience. Thermaxhad to pay a heavy penalty for not finding a suitable successor, as in less than 5 years time, Therrnaxs sales have fallen from 990.45 crore in 1996 to 185.88 crore in 2000. (Bolar) More or less, similar situation prevailed in most private sector companies where family members have been routinely crowned with top-level positions for a fairly long time. In a family - managed organisation the joke was that managers came there vertically but went out horizontally! (not leavirig any room for others till they died). The situation in Thermax, for example, was remedied only recently when Anu Aga suddenly decided to step down, making way for professional managers at the top. Thanks to the competition from global giants and many other private sector companies have realised the importance of professional managers at the top-level.To this end, the CEO-designate (mostly sons and daughters) is not only sent abroad for top-class training but alsomade to undergo training at various levels within the organisation (Apollo Hospitals, Dr. Reddy Bajaj Auto, etc.)

**Reasons for not having a Succession Plan**

The reasons for the temperamental aversion towards succession planning

may be stated thus:

1.Why to commit the company to a CEO-select years in advance; he may create a scare, abuse the power, pose a threat to other talented people; open up a second line of command and begin to create a powerful lobby for himself. .

2.It is better to weed out all possible successors, so that (the present incumbent) I can have a smooth run.

3.Nobody is really capable enough to take charge as yet. As long as I am here, there is no need to search for talent anywhere else.

Post-liberalisation, of course, many private setter companies have realised the importance of grooming bright stars well in advance, internally (including the Tatas, the 'Birlas, Bajaj Auto, Ranbaxy and many others).

**Why Succession Planning Fails ?**

1. High potential candidates are arbitrarily identified.
2. The qualities that a successful business unit head has and what he should have as a CEO after promotion are different. Business unit heads may not have strategic vision or the ability to communicate effectively with external stakeholders.
3. Many executives make excellent No. 2s and act as a fine complement to their CEOs but fail miserably when they move into the corner office.
4. The designated replacement may be far from ready to take over. The evaluation may be more positive than what it should be.
5. Promotions are made keeping in view the organizational needs, but totally ignoring the employee aspirations.
6. The process lacks transparency and confuses talented people who may decide to leave.
7. Outside hires are brought in indiscriminately without explaining the rationale to insiders. 8.When one person leaves, instead of moving decisively and appointing a successor, the portfolio is split among two people at the next level, leaving people totally confused (Ved Puriswar). The program is perceived as being limited to the elite core!

**Guidelines for effective succession planning**

1.Succession Planning should be of the organization customized to suit the needs. For example, if the skills necessary to manage the company in the changed environment are not available in house, there may be no option but to bring in an outsider.

2.Succession planning should be driven by the line function and not HR cxccutivcs.

3.Succession planning should develop key candidates, in anticipation of future openings.

4.Succession planning is not just selection. Development through job rotation, mentoring and formal training programs is equally ·important.

5.Succession planning must take into account the culture of the organization.

6.Succession planning must be consistent with the future strategic direction of the company.

**Succession Management**

Succession management, an alternative approach developed in the 1990s, is used to examine existing managerial talent in light of future competencies and future business needs and challenges. The basic purpose of succession management is to ensure that the right talent is available when needed and that appropriate development experiences are provided for higher-level employees. It focuses on creating and stocking pools of candidates with high leadership potential. To this end, it may even track non-employees (for example, employees of a competitor) whom the organisation views as viable candidates should a position open up.

Another difference between succession planning and succession management is the emphasis put on ensuring that planned training and development actually takes place. Very often, succession plans do not go beyond identifying potential successors. The required developmental experience and rich training inputs may not be flowing in readily. Succession management assures that key people are not just identified but also nurtured and developed into future leadership roles (both terms, are however, used interchangeably in this text.

Succession management includes the following activities: (Leihaman)

1. ___Identifying the shortage of leadership skills and defining the Requirements___: With a view to identifying the impending shortage of leadership skills, organisations have to estimate manpower requirements well in advance. HR professionals generally estimate manpower flows, using various forecasting techniques. In respect of a commercial bank, for example skill shortages may arise due to retirement, resignation, transfer, VRS schemes, etc.,

This has to be followed by a clear-cut workload analysis to define the executive competencies required at various levels. Competencies may be defined by focusing attention on the Bank's critical success factors and values and the challenges it expects to face in the next five years and beyond. These would include, for instance, diversification plans into areas such as insurance, credit cards, auto finance, consumer finance, housing finance etc., and the competencies needed to filL the skill shortages. Managerial judgement and a careful study of the past· trends may serve as a useful guide in this regard.

**_2.Identifying potential successors for critical positions_**: Once shortages are assessed and skill requirements defined, the next step is to find people with requisite talent to move into senior leadership roles. To find people. with the highest potential, the organisation has to collect information from various sources (search every division/subsidiary): how they performed in the past on various jobs, feedback from subordinates, customers, etc., regarding their key skill competencies and core values, etc.

One organisation looking for potential top leaders asked its managers to go through an extensive assessment centre programme, where outside professional experts offered an accurate, unbiased view of the potential of trainees. Other methods such as aptitude tests, projective tests, interest tests, ana simulation exercises could also be used to assess the potential of candidates with lots of promise.

Since it is not possible to 'fasttrack' everyone, it is always better to define the critical success factors of important jobs initially and evaluate the high-potential successors against those benchmarks. Success factors are the behaviours required to perform the identified jobs successfully in the organisation's culture. The thumb rule is that ten per cent of all managerial positions are critical. Once that has been done, it is advisable to have at least two identified successors for each of the critical positions. However, if the identified candidates are not yet ready to take the challenges head-on, it may be a good idea to train them further.

**_2.Coach and groom the 'stars'_**; After identifying potential successors for important positions, the organisation must devise ways and means to fast track their development. Enriching developmental opportunities must be thrown open to them such as handling two important projects, a foreign country assignment, a major market research job, a new product launch, a complex industrial relations exercise etc. The methods must be tailor-made to suit the mental make-up of candidates and, at the same, allow the candidates to improve the targeted behaviours.

The identified high-fliers should be continually challenged and developed with demanding jobs intended to stretch their leadership competencies and enrich their experiences. At various levels, conscious efforts must be made to make fast trackers know how important they are in the organisation's future plans. The organisation should not let talent walk out of the door. Appropriate retention strategies must be devised in time so that a competitor or a dot. com does not poach the 'identified stars.'

**_4.Secure top management's commitment and support_**: The above development-oriented action plan would be fruitless if it does not enjoy consistent support and continued blessings from top management. Executive assessment, training, development and retention programmes, after all, demand lot of support from 'upstairs' .

**Current Scenario : a study**

Succession planning is an issue of strategic importance demanding the time and attention of top management on an ongoing basis. Top management should take up the issue of finding a suitable and worthy successor in a proactive manner. Hindustan Lever is an excellent example in this regard (Business India, 9th August 2009) Throughout its glorious histoty in India, there has been no case of any CEO failing to deliver results. At HUL, in fact, for every key position, there are at least three different names-and these are drop-dead succession people who can take over at a moment's notice-according to Leena Nair ED(HR) Most private sector companies--especially the family businesses-have been waking up to the challenge and preparing themselves for the baton change in a systematic manner. Ratan Tata-over 73 now - has to hang up his boots some day but in the Tara Group there is no practice of naming CEOs in advance. Tara companies believe in allowing people room to grow. The Group has over 60 companies that need CEOs. Mostly a potential candidate is expected to cut his teeth in a smaller company before moving on to larger assignments. The Ambanis, the Birlas and many more family owned organisations are slowly bur steadily preparing their recipes for the new environment. Apart from acquiring professional qualifications, the potential candidates are made to work through their way to the top-undergoing training for a minimum period of at least five years. Roshni Nadar has just been made theCEO of HCL Group. Parle Agro's Prakash Chauhan has passed the baton to daughter Shauna Chauhan with her two sisters as supporting cast. At Bisleri, Ramesh Chauhan is abour to hand over charge to daughter Jayanti Chauhan. Prathap Reddy of Apollo Hospitals has all four of his daughters at the business. Pia Singh, daughter of K.P. Singh heads the DLF's entertainment and retail ventures. TCS has ensured a smooth transition from Ramadorai to Chandrasekaran in 2009. Azim Premji of Wipro boasts of a clear succession plan in place-and his eldest son Rishad is being groomed carefully for the top job in the interim. Other groups - such as the Piramal, the Jindal, the Godrej, the Murugappa, the Goenkas, etc-have more or less realized the importance of separating ownership from management. The transfer of power in Il?:0[st] private sector banks in India also has been smooth. For example at ICICI bank there has been a practically seamless transfer of power from K.Y. Kamath to Chanda Kochhar-as earlier from N. Vaghul to Kamath. The same, however, cannot be said in case of public sector units (PSUs) in India. Many of these posts are either unfilled or manned by bureaucrats named by the Government. Most CEOs, not surprisingly, -spend more time in protecting their -turf rather than grooming talent for the next line of leadership. To ensure a smooth and successful transition, of course, this kind of knee jerk reactions and adhoc decisions must be dispensed with. Over time, all enterprises evolve and grow around the vision, skill and enthusiasm of the people who lead and manage them. The business gradually becomes an embodiment of their judgement, values and decisions. If they retire or .exit for other reasons, the ethos and dynamics of the business will inevitably change.' If the value of the business is to be maintained or enhanced, it is essential to keep.the checklist for a smooth and painless baton change.

## How to Deal with CEO-churn?

CEOs today are unlikely to remain in office for quite as long as their predecessors, Luc Vandesvelde was CEO of Marks & Spencer for just three years. Louis Camilleri held the top spot at Philip Morris for only two years, while Greg Dyke was Chairman at the BBC for just two years too. In fact over the past five years, around two-thirds of all major companies worldwide replaced their bosses and that CEO tenure has decreased sharply. Job security for CEOs globally is diminishing. In virtually every industry CEO turnover is rising and leadership changes are occurring more frequently. If these trends continue, they , will have a significant impact on executive careers and how organisations are managed. As CEO tenure is reduced, a growing number of leaders will be required to implement their plans and strategies within more limited time frames, reinforcing the current corporate focus on short-term business results. Despite these changes, many companies still tend to look for CEO successors with extensive company experience within their own ranks. So whilst many companies feel the need to change leaders more often, they still place a high value on executive continuity and stability Because of the complex nature of corporations today, it is also not surprising that corporate boards prefer candidates to have come from inside the business because they tend to have market, product, technical, organisational and cultural knowledge that's required.

## An Example of Succession Management: Bajaj Auto

The belief that 'tomorrow's CEO must be today's empowered manager' compelled 57-year old Rahul Bajaj, CEO of the two-wheeler giant Bajaj Auto, to delegate his responsibility to a successor systematically, in early 90s. Both the heirs apparent - his two sons Rajiv and Sanjiv - are qualified enough to exchange the baton smoothly. (Bikram Chhachhi) For a man who took charge of every critical area in the traditionally family-managed company, the decision is a bold one. He assumed complete charge of production, finance, design changes, production systems, and labour relations at the company, personally overseeing all operations for over two decades (1968-1990).

He never realised the need for delegation of authority and decentralisation of responsibilities. Not surprisingly, the company remained a fat, cost-callous, inflexible giant although rising sales and burgeoning consumer demand camouflaged the flab. The second-line of executives were never groomed to manage at least day-to-day operations. He never allowed others the required freedom to take even simple decisions independently. Additional responsibilities as the Chairman of Indian Airlines, CII, AIAM, etc., literally forced him to discount the value of creating a second line of command in his absence. meanwhile, with the onset of a recession and the advent of competition, the company had to rewrite the rules of the game quickly, combining delegation with succession planning. The process of succession management planned by Rahul Bajaj involved the following steps:

**Arm your successor**: Both sons joined as apprentices initially. They were allowed to choose their respective focus areas and then undergo intensive training in those areas: Rajiv in manufacturing and Sanjiv in marketing. Another cousin of Rahul Bajaj, Madhur was made the in-charge of HR functions and began to represent Rahul in company meetings. '

**Begin at the edges**: Responsibilities were delegated to Madhur slowly but steadily, allowing the successor enough time to adjust to new siruations and challenges.

**Start succession early**: On his return from Warwick University, Rajiv was given charge of the Akurdi Plant and allowed to decide things independently. Strategic decisions, however, were discussed by both father and son thoroughly and actions initiated only when both were satisfied by the underlying logic.

**Prepare the organisation**: Rahul started distancing himself from his followers as the process began in the early 90s. He, thus, made the workers adjust to the successor's ways of doing things. The gradual withdrawal was consciously planned so that the inheritor can 'have his own brand of management style. The report card of the company, after effecting all these changes smoothly, is excellent in that the three successors have been able to push competitors to the wall and show far superior performance year after year.

**LESSONS OF SUCCESS FROM LEADERS**

<u>Leadership</u> is learned behavior that becomes unconscious and automatic over time. For example, leaders can make several important decisions about an issue in the time it takes others to understand the question. Many people wonder how leaders know how to make the best decisions, often under immense pressure. The process of making these decisions comes from an accumulation of experiences and encounters with a multitude of difference circumstances, personality types and unforeseen failures. More so, the decision making process is an acute understanding of being familiar with the cause and effect of behavioral and circumstantial patterns; knowing the intelligence and interconnection points of the variables involved in these patterns allows a leader to confidently make decisions and project the probability of their desired outcomes. The most successful leaders are instinctual decision makers. Having done it so many times throughout their careers, they become immune to the pressure associated with decision making and extremely intuitive about the process of making the most strategic and best decisions. This is why most senior executives will tell you they depend strongly upon their "gut-feel" when making difficult decisions at a moment's notice.

Beyond decision making, successful leadership across all areas becomes learned and instinctual over a period of time. Successful leaders have learned the mastery of anticipating business patterns, finding opportunities in pressure situations, serving the people they lead and overcoming hardships. No wonder the best CEOs are paid so much money. In 2011, salaries for the 200 top-paid CEOs rose 5 percent to a median $14.5 million per year, according to a study by compensation-data company Equilar for <u>The New York Times</u>.

If you are looking to advance your career into a leadership capacity and / or already assume leadership responsibilities – here are 15 things you must do automatically, every day, to be a successful leader in the workplace:

**1. Make Others Feel Safe to Speak-Up**

Many times leaders intimidate their colleagues with their title and power when they walk into a room. Successful leaders deflect attention away from themselves and encourage others to voice their opinions. They are experts at making <u>others feel safe to speak-up</u> and confidently share their perspectives and points of view. They use their <u>executive presence</u> to create an approachable environment.

**2. Make Decisions**

Successful leaders are expert decision makers. They either facilitate the dialogue to empower their colleagues to reach a strategic conclusion or they do it themselves. They focus on "making things happen" at all times – decision making activities that sustain progress. Successful leaders have mastered the art of politicking and thus don't waste their time on issues that disrupt momentum. <u>They know how to make 30 decisions in 30 minutes</u>.

### 3. Communicate Expectations

Successful leaders are great communicators, and this is especially true when it comes to "performance expectations." In doing so, they remind their colleagues of the organization's core values and mission statement – ensuring that their vision is properly translated and actionable objectives are properly executed.

I had a boss that managed the team by reminding us of the expectations that she had of the group. She made it easy for the team to stay focused and on track. The protocol she implemented – by clearly communicating expectations – increased performance and helped to identify those on the team that could not keep up with the standards she expected from us.

### 4. Challenge People to Think

The most successful leaders understand their colleagues' mindsets, capabilities and areas for improvement. They use this knowledge/insight to challenge their teams to think and stretch them to reach for more. These types of leaders excel in keeping their people on their toes, never allowing them to get comfortable and enabling them with the tools to grow.

If you are not thinking, you're not learning new things. If you're not learning, you're not growing – and over time becoming irrelevant in your work.

### 5. Be Accountable to Others

Successful leaders allow their colleagues to manage them. This doesn't mean they are allowing others to control them – but rather becoming accountable to assure they are being proactive to their colleagues needs.

Beyond just mentoring and sponsoring selected employees, being accountable to others is a sign that your leader is focused more on your success than just their own.

### 6. Lead by Example

Leading by example sounds easy, but few leaders are consistent with this one. Successful leaders practice what they preach and are mindful of their actions. They know everyone is watching them and therefore are incredibly intuitive about detecting those who are observing their every move, waiting to detect a performance shortfall.

**7. Measure & Reward Performance**

Great leaders always have a strong "pulse" on business performance and those people who are the performance champions. Not only do they review the numbers and measure performance ROI, they are active in acknowledging hard work and efforts (no matter the result). Successful leaders never take consistent performers for granted and are mindful of rewarding them. **8. Provide Continuous Feedback**

Employees want their leaders to know that they are paying attention to them and they appreciate any insights along the way. Successful leaders always provide feedback and they welcome reciprocal feedback by creating trustworthy relationships with their colleagues.. They understand the power of perspective and have learned the importance of feedback early on in their career as it has served them to enable workplace advancement.

**9. Properly Allocate and Deploy Talent**

Successful leaders know their talent pool and how to use it. They are experts at activating the capabilities of their colleagues and knowing when to deploy their unique skill sets given the circumstances at hand.

**10. Ask Questions, Seek Counsel**

Successful leaders ask questions and seek counsel all the time. From the outside, they appear to know-it-all – yet on the inside, they have a deep thirst for knowledge and constantly are on the look-out to learn new things because of their commitment to making themselves better through the wisdom of othe

**11. Problem Solve; Avoid Procrastination**

Successful leaders tackle issues head-on and know how to discover the heart of the matter at hand. They don't procrastinate and thus become incredibly proficient at problem solving; they learn from and don't avoid uncomfortable circumstances (they welcome them).

Getting ahead in life is about doing the things that most people don't like doing.

**12. Positive Energy & Attitude**

Successful leaders create a positive and inspiring workplace culture. They know how to set the tone and bring an attitude that motivates their colleagues to take action. As such, they are likeable, respected and strong willed. They don't allow failures to disrupt momentum.

**13. Be a Great Teacher**

Many employees in the workplace will tell you that their leaders have stopped being teachers. Successful leaders never stop teaching because they are so self-motivated to learn themselves. They use teaching to keep their colleagues well-informed and knowledgeable through statistics, trends, and other newsworthy items.

Successful leaders take the time to mentor their colleagues and make the investment to sponsor those who have proven they are able and eager to advance.

### 14. Invest in Relationships

Successful leaders don't focus on protecting their domain – instead they expand it by investing in mutually beneficial relationships. Successful leaders associate themselves with "lifters and other leaders" – the types of people that can broaden their sphere of influence. Not only for their own advancement, but that of others.

Leaders share the harvest of their success to help build momentum for those around them.

### 15. Genuinely Enjoy Responsibilities

Successful leaders love being leaders – not for the sake of power but for the meaningful and purposeful impact they can create. When you have reached a senior level of leadership – it's about your ability to serve others and this can't be accomplished unless you genuinely enjoy what you do.

In the end, successful leaders are able to sustain their success because these 15 things ultimately allow them to increase the value of their organization's brand – while at the same time minimize the operating risk profile. They serve as the enablers of talent, culture and results

Napoleon Hill's list of key attributes that serves as a success for leaders:

1. Self confidence, be knowledgeable about your work
2. Self control, remain calm under pressure
3. Sense of justice, fairness & respect for others
4. Decisive and stand by decisions
5. Organization & planning skills
6. Strong work ethic
7. Neatness & hygiene
8. Empathy
9. Mastery of details
10. True accountability in deed as well as word
11. The ability to achieve through others

## LESSONS OF FAILURES FROM THE LEADERS

**The first cause of failure** is the inability to organize details. According to Hill "efficient leadership calls for (the) ability to organize and to master details. No genuine leader is ever too busy to do anything which may be required of him in his capacity as leader. When a man, whether he is a leader or follower, admits that he is too busy to change his plans, or to give attention to any emergency, he admits his inefficiency. The successful leader must be the master of all details connected with his position. That means, of course, that he must acquire the habit of relegating details to capable lieutenants". This failure relates to two key skills required by the successful leader or Project Manager – good organization skills, and the ability to delegate effectively. Too many managers create a project plan at the start of the project, and then do no more than tick it off, as if the project plan can manage the project. A good leader or manager is across the details of the plan, and manages it effectively.

Even more disheartening is the manager who abdicates responsibility rather than delegating responsibility. What's the difference you might ask? When a task is delegated to someone, consideration is given to the person's skills and ability to do the task, the amount of supervision required, and their capacity to do the task. The manager keeps track of the task, and assists where necessary. When a task is abdicated, it is farmed off to the nearest person without regards to their capacity, skills and knowledge (and therefore ability to do the job) and with no follow up, save for blaming the poor soul when the task invariably fails, as it must.

**The second cause of failure** according to Hill is the "unwillingness to render humble service. Truly great leaders are willing, when occasion demands, to perform any sort of labour which they would ask another to perform ". This is the corollary of success attribute number 6 – strong work ethic. No manager can be truly successful if they ask more of others than they are willing to do themselves, or if they consistently delegate the most odious tasks to more junior staff.

**The third cause of failure** is an "expectation of pay for what they know instead of what they do with that which they know. The world does not pay men for that which they know. It pays them for what they do, or induce others to do". This one brought a smile to my face, for I have met many managers and so-called leaders who expect remuneration and respect because they have been in a job for so many years, or they have an MBA or they know influential people. It's not what you know or who you know – it's what you actually do that counts!

**The fourth cause of failure** is "fear of competition from followers". Hill goes on to state that "the leader who fears that one of his followers may take his position is practically sure to realize that fear sooner or later". No leader can lead who is continually looking back over his or her shoulder to see who is gaining on them. Great leaders and managers encourage and nurture good people and enjoy working with them.

Someone once told me that you should never be indispensable – as a manager you should always make sure that one of your direct reports is capable and able of taking over from you at a moment's notice. This means that you need to nurture them, train and mentor them, and trust them. This benefits not only them, but you, should a better opportunity open up.

**The fifth cause of failure** is lack of imagination. According to Hill "without imagination, the leader is incapable of meeting emergencies, and of creating plans by which to guide his followers efficiently". Sadly to say, many Project Managers today seem to think that Project Management is a paint by numbers job – build a project plan and then everything will run along tickety-boo. It doesn't, and it doesn't help if the Project Manager cannot keep their head in a crisis, modify project plans, risks and issues on the fly, and quickly ascertain viable alternatives when the project is in crisis.

**The sixth cause of failure** is selfishness. Hill goes on to say "the leader who claims all the honour for the work of his followers is sure to be met by resentment. The really great leader claims none of the honours. He is contented to see the honours, when there are any, go to his followers, because he knows that most men will work harder for commendation and recognition than they will for money alone". And funny how those managers who do "steal all the glory" are the self same ones who never accept responsibility or take the blame, even for the most minor of problems.

**The seventh cause of failure**, according to Hill, is intemperance. By intemperance, Hill refers to over indulgence in any pleasures, be they food, drink, drugs, gambling or sex. Hill believed that "followers do not respect an intemperate leader. Moreover, intemperance, in any of its various forms, destroys the endurance and the vitality of all who indulge in it". Whilst this may seem somewhat quaint today, I think the point he was trying to make is that a great leader does not have time to over indulge in anything (the key being over indulge). A truly great leader always has his or her eyes on the prize!

**The eight cause of failure** is disloyalty. According to Hill, "the leader who is not loyal to his trust, and to his associates, those above him, and those below him, cannot long maintain his leadership". A manager who does not trust and respect their team will find the going very tough if they need to call for extra effort from the team.

**The ninth cause of failure** is an emphasis on the "authority" of leadership. Here, Hill is referring to those leaders and managers who manage through fear and intimidation, rather than respect. Those "I am the boss and you'll do what I say" types (and yes, they still exist). Hill goes on to say "the efficient leader leads by encouraging, and not by trying to instil fear in the hearts of his followers. ... If a leader is a real leader, he will have no need to advertise that fact except by his conduct - his sympathy, understanding, fairness, and a demonstration that he knows his job".

**The tenth and final causeof failure** is an emphasis on title. This touches on the subject of positional versus personal authority. A great leader or project manager has personal authority – if they were to be demoted to the lowest rank, they would still have the respect of their peers (and superiors) due to their personal authority. However, many managers rely on positional authority – such as a grand title (Executive Vice President or Corporate Change Manager) or the fact that they report directly to the Board of Directors. Remove them from that role and they are nothing! According to Hill "the competent leader requires no "title" to give him the respect of his followers. The man who makes too much over his title generally has little else to emphasize".

In summary, then, the major causes of failure in leadership are:

1. Inability to organize details
2. Unwillingness to do that which you ask of others
3. Expectation of pay for what you know rather than what you do
4. Fear of competition
5. Lack of imagination
6. Selfishness
7. Intemperance, over indulgence
8. Disloyalty
9. Emphasis on the "authority" of leadership
10. Emphasis on title

## CASE STUDY

## THE LIFE AND TIMES OF JAYALALITHA

MISJUDGED, misled, misinterpreted, misunderstood and mismanaged. All this, say her friends, has rendered J. Jayalalitha highly unpredictable,

The disenchantment with practically everyone she was close to is reflected in her autobiography published in the Tamil weekly Kumudam in 1978. Her father is presented as a "squanderer and a gentleman of leisure", a man "who could not handle anything properly". MGR is a person who she said she would rather "treat as an equal rather than a superstar". A 'betrayal' by a school friend too left a deep impression. Jayalalitha had played postman for this friend who was in love with a neighbour. But "when the girl's mother discovered what was going on, my friend played Brutus and painted me as a daughter of an actress and a girl of loose morals."

This overwhelming sense of being 'used' seems to have influenced the worldview of the otherwise precocious and sensitive girl who dreamed of "becoming a millionaire and a lawyer", collected pictures of Rock Hudson and had a crush on cricketers Nari Contractor and Mansur Ali Khan Pataudi.

"I used to go for matches with binoculars just to look at Pataudi and Pataudi alone," she croons. Her dream world collapsed when her mother Sandhya—also an actress known to MGR—revealed that a "financial crisis in the family" meant that 'Jay' would have to give up studies and start acting. Recalls Jayal-alitha: "It was a rude shock to me. My argument with Amma was that it was she who punished me for putting on make-up and told me to stay off cinema who was now pushing me into acting."

So the 16-year-old, instead of going to Stella Maris College, went to the sets of director C.V. Sridhar's film Vennira Aadai (Widow's Robe). An ironic title for a woman who never married, although she confesses she never understood "the word platonic" and believed that "either there is a romantic relationship between two people or they are just friends". A loner, Jayalalitha seems to have harboured a distrust for others rather early in life. "The experiences I have been through, the suffering and pain have taught me an important lesson: in life there is one person you must rely on—yourself."

Her former friends have all been abandoned. Cho Ramaswamy, editor of Tughlaq who she fondly describes in her autobiography as a 'valuable' friend, was recently admonished publicly and asked "not to describe himself as a friend". Salem Kannan, two-time AIADMK MP who virtually created a political base for her in the party, is now persona non grata. Ministers in MGR's cabinet and former Jaya loyalists S. Thirunavakkarsu and K.K.S.S.R

Ramachandran have been eased out of the party. Says Kannan: "After all that I have done for her, I am deeply hurt at the manner in which she dumped me when I advised her to keep Sasikala and her family at a distance."

Kannan and Valampuri John were privy to her blow-hot-blow-cold relationship with MGR. According to John, MGR was 'suspicious' of Jayalalitha and monitored her every move. He realised that she was a very independent woman "who acted on her own volition". Indeed, when

MGR had reasons to be suspicious. In late 1984 when he was hospitalised in the US following a stroke, Jayalalitha, a Rajya Sabha MP since 1983, was convinced that she should take over the reins. She approached the then prime minister, Rajiv Gandhi, and governor S.L. Khurana to appoint her chief minister since she felt that MGR's health would not permit him to discharge his duties. Her moves were widely reported. Kannan who acted as her courier confirms her efforts to get to the top slot. So does John. Thirunavakkarsu. And R.M. Veerappan.

Stung by her moves, MGR stripped her of the deputy leadership of the parliamentary party. In an interview to Savvy magazine, she articulated her anger against the decision: "MGR has been a great influence in my life, I don't deny that. But now I am my own person. I have evolved. Hereafter, I am responsible only for myself. Never again will anybody influence me to such an extent that all my thoughts and actions and statements are influenced and made in a particular way just because someone else wants it that way."

According to Jayalalitha's inner circle, it was her success in managing MGR, often described as the wiliest of CMs, that convinced her she could manipulate all categories of politicians. Her pressure tactics with the BJP, they aver, are only a manifestation of this. Her former friend Thirunavakkarsu notes: "She has a history of using people and then discarding them." According to him, she has no permanent friends. This perhaps explains why she has tied up with her one-time arch rival Subramanian Swamy. Adds Thirunavakkarsu: "You cannot view her actions through traditional logic. She is a very impulsive person who manufactures situations to push her own personal agenda."

To a great degree, MGR is responsible for her achieving instant VIP status in the party. It was he who gave orders to partymen that they should stand up to show their respect to her. It was he who advised her to shun the media. When she came to power in 1991, she took all this to an extreme limit. She kept even her ministers at a distance. It was widely believed that it was Sasikala Natarajan who ran the government.

Political wisdom dictates that Jayalalitha should be more diplomatic. But Jayalalitha functions on the principle, what Jaya wants Jaya shall get.

# CHAPTER SIX

# BUSINESS PROCESS OUTSOURCING

## 6.1 BPO

BPO stands for Business Process Outsourcing. BPO in a general term used to describe the outsourcing of critical, but non-core, business processes or functions of an organization to external vendors for certain period on a set of predefined performance metrices.

It is the contracting of a specific business task, such as payroll, to a third-party service provider. BPO is handing over a particular Business Process to a Third Party Service Provider.

For example a Company whose primary business is to manufacture and sell computers might hire a Company to handle calls of it's customers for servicing and repair works.

In this case the Company which is handling the incoming calls of customers is a nothing but a BPO Company which is taking up a process of another company.

BPO is typically categorised into Back Office outsourcing - which may include business functions like Human Resource, Finance, Accounting, Email etc and Front Office outsourcing - which may include Customer Service, Complaints, Contact Center etc.

**Benefits of BPO –**

The Outsourcing market is growing tremendously in the coming few with increasing years with an increasing advantage as discussed below:-

**1. Productivity improvement:**

BPO enables to the corporate executive to concentrate upon core business areas. Conventionally executives spend more time in management of details and they get very little time to formulate strategies. BPO saves time and helps the executives to explore new revenue areas, accelerate other projects and focus on their customers. This leads to improvement in the productivity. Better educated or skilled people perform the task efficiently and thus improve productivity.

**2. Optimum utilisation of the resources:**

BPO enables optimum utilisation of resources of scarce resources. Outsourcing helps to capture new efficiencies and reallocate the resources. This increases the efficiency and productivity. Availability of skilled employees and adoption of sophisticated technologies leads to utilisation of resources and productivity.

**3. Reduction in cost:**

Cost savings can be significant to any business. BPO not only helps in reducing cost but also increase productivity and raise revenue significantly. Cost reduction is possible through process improvements, reengineering, and use of technologies that reduce and bring administrative and other costs under control. Outsourcing helps the company maintain lower rates with better service solutions, thereby giving them a better market position and even a competitive advantage.

**4. Improved Human Resource:**

Improved HR is another great advantage of outsourcing business processes. Cost effective manpower is yet another important factor of importance in BPO. Companies today, require productive and efficient human resource that can generate economies of scale. Due to outsourcing business can save Human resource cost, depending on their priorities. Outsourcing gives a company the ability to get access to skilled and trained man power at extremely low rates

**5. Focus on core business areas:**

Efficient business strategy is essential to take the business to the top. Outsourcing enables the top management level to hand over critical but non-core activities of the business to the third party. This facilitates top management level to concentrate on the core activities.

**6. Cater to changing customer demands:**

It is another great advantage of outsourcing the business processes. Many BPOs provide the management with flexible services to meet the customers' changing requirements, and to support company acquisitions, consolidations, and joint ventures.

**7. Sophisticated technology at lower cost:**

Technology is the leading area of outsourcing. It makes much of the work of modern organisation easy. Investing in new technology is very costly and often risky. As the technology market develops rapidly, it is difficult to keep pace with the latest innovations and solutions. Thus outsourcing to companies that have the resources, expertise and desire to continuously update their technological solutions, offers a true advantage of outsourcing.

## 6.2 BPO MODELS AND TYPES OF VENDORS

Service providers who undertake the responsibility of performing such activities can either offer only few of the outsourcing activities or a more end to end services encompassing of much larger range of activities. This depends on the capabilities developed by such BPO vendors and the scale at which the vendor operates.

BPO services have three kinds of business model depending on the type of activities handled by them. These are as follows:

1. Transactional
2. Niche and
3. Comprehensive

**Transactional**: Transactional providers typically handle only one process and not the entire activity. They are at the low end of the value chain.

For example: In Payroll, the BPO vendors will not take over the entire department but will be responsible for only one activity, like cutting cheques.

Such contracts are short generally annual or less than 2 years. And have less contract value. Performance metrics are decided per transaction and the company has total control over the whole process and has to develop an in-house department to monitor it. Generally occurs in initial stages of BPO.

**Niche:** Niche providers handle a wider range or sequence of transactions, typically 2 or 4 processes. But they still don't handle the entire activity. These deals tend to be 3 or more years. And the contract value is also more than the transactional providers. They have good domain knowledge and are also effect productivity and quality improvements over a period of time. They aim to make selected processes more efficient by lowering costs for the companies and raising service levels.

**Comprehensive:** Comprehensive providers handle almost all the transactional and administrative processes in a function.

For example: Handling of entire HR function – which includes all the 22 activities.

They are typically long term contracts, 10 yrs and look for global deals. The value of this type of contract is very high and goes in billions of dollars. Comprehensive vendors have ability to make interrelated functions more efficient by introducing best practices, thereby reducing the total cost of a function. They are completely responsible and accountable for the entire function.

Example – Exult (since acquired by HP)

Interestingly, Transactional services providers act as sub contractors for Niche service providers and both act as sub-contractors to Comprehensive service providers. They effectively act as Tier III, Tier II and Tier I outsourcers.

BPO vendors can be classified into three distinct types depending on the history or origin of the company, expertise etc.

1. Traditional IT services/IT Outsourcing companies: these companies have a good track of services in traditional IT areas. Companies such as IBM, Global Services, Unisys, Infosys, Wipro, TCS etc fall into this category. They have started offering their expertise and client relationships that are already in existence.

2. Consulting firms: these companies have distinct advantage of working with several companies and are hence exposed to the best practices followed worldwide. They also help in re-engineer processes and helps in reducing cost. Their domain knowledge gives them tremendous competitive advantage to build CEO level relationships over a period of time. Companies such as Hewitt, Accenture, Ernst and young are come consulting firms.

3. Pure Play BPO Vendors: these companies are setup exclusively for undertaking BPO contracts. Such companies have grown over a period of time relatively lower end Transaction BPO and Niche BPOs. The growth is in the areas like transcription, call centre's, e-accounts etc.

**Healthcare BPO**

Healthcare BPO industry involves outsourcing activities related to creation, maintenance and exchange of patient information between healthcare providers (Hospitals, Physicians, clinics, Pharmacies etc) and the healthcare payers such as insurance companies. Some of the healthcare services include

Medical transcription: conversion of medical data from speech or handwritten format to electronic form

Document management: Collation of patients' medical and demographic record into a single computerized patient record with database and e-signature functionalities.

Coding: Assigning the predefined diagnostic and treatment codes to different medical procedures

Billing: Combining patient records, codes and charge sheets to generate claims/bills.

Form processing: scanning of handwritten documents, converting them into electronic form and sending it back.

Receivable management: Follow-up and collection of receivables.

Company health analysis: medical history of all employees of a company is analyzed to find out the health risk of a company.

List of some MT companies in India:

CBay Systems, Healthscribe, Heartland, Microgenetics, Saral Infotech, Medsoft, Mediscribe etc.

**Transaction Processing BPO**

Most of the organizations around the world face the tedious task of processing countless transaction to record day to day activities that they perform in the process of providing goods and services to their customers. They need to generate, manage and document multiple forms in an organized, accessible manner. They then need to process the data according to a set of pre-defined rules, often with the use of computers. Output data from one process acts as the input data for another process. This series of rule based data processing is called transaction processing.

Transaction processing includes Banking transactions, credit and card processing, mortgage processing, claims processing and horizontal areas like basic accounting, receivables management, accounts payables etc.

Companies outsource these activities which are repetitive and they can in turn focus on enhancing their core competencies and serving their customers better.

Some of the reasons why companies prefer outsourcing such transactions intensive activities are :

- This high cost of transactions
- Too much time spent on daily operations

- The high cost of upgrading applications
- Difficulty in hiring and retaining the high quality process staff
- Inability to put best practices and performance parameters in place.

**Human Resource BPO**

The HR department is critical for employee well-being in any business no matter how small the business is. A motivated and innovative employee can work wonders for a marketplace. HR outsourcing is defined as the process of outsourcing the HR activities to a third party having expertise in HR field.

The typical services include:

- Payroll administration: producing cheques, handling taxes, dealing with sick time and vacation time
- Employee benefits: Health and medical life, 401(k) plans, cafeteria etc
- HR management: Recruiting, hiring and firing, background interviews, exit and wage interviews
- Risk Management: Workers' compensation, dispute resolution, safety inspection, Office policies and handbooks.

**Offshoring**

Many corporations in the developed countries did not feel that the cost of benefit of outsourcing to a service provider located in their own country was not worth their while. The following terms are used to indicate the location of the service providers

1. Onshore: In case the service provider is located on the shore i.e if the US based company is outsourcing to another US based company, the process will be called onshoring.
2. Near-shoring: In case the service provider is located near the shore in a lower cost country location in nearby countries. For example: if a US based company outsources to another company based in Canada, the process is called near shoring.
3. Off shore: In case the service provider is located far away from the company which is outsourcing work and the communication and control is exerted using IT enable tools over long distance telecom networks. For example: if a US based company outsources work to another company based in India, the process is called offshoring.

The dominant role in the birth of offshoring can be credited to rise of Information Technology, reduction in networking costs and internet. Offshoring in the manufacturing industry accelerated in a big way with two events. The first event was the signing of NAFTA (North American Free Trade Agreement) in 1993, which gave boost to the process of offshoring. The second event was 1994 passage of GATT (General Agreement on Trade and Tariffs) further accelerated its opened door policy towards investment and a new aspect of outsourcing emerged.

Many multinational companies preferred to outsource work to India and other Asian Countries such as Philippines, Malaysia etc. since they offered unique combination of low costs and quality manpower.

**6.3 BPO IN INDIA**

Due to the open market and the demand for outsourcing, more and more BPO companies in India are setting up bases in various parts of the country. Most of these companies cater to the global MNCs, banks and so on. The business process outsourcing sector is one of the booming industries in the country and more and more young professionals are joining it to earn good salary.

According to the recent surveys, the BPO industry provides employment to around 0.7 million people across the country. The yearly revenue amounts to around $11 billion with a share of around 1 % of the annual Gross Domestic Product (GDP). The BPO industry is also a lucrative option for both graduates and freshers as one can get good salary. The growth rate of the wages and salaries in the sector range from 10-15 % every year.

There are also well known domestic BPO companies which cater to the national as well as the international market. Some of the cities where the business processing industry is popular are Chennai, Bangalore, Hyderabad, Kolkata, New Delhi, and Mumbai and so on. To cater to the growing demand, more BPO companies are also setting up bases in other cities across the country like Pune, Gurgaon, Coimbatore, Kochi, Chandigarh, Bhubaneshwar, and Lucknow and so on.

## *Leading BPO companies in India*

The BPO companies are judged according to the clients they cater to, their work and the output and also the employee welfare and satisfaction. Based on these, some of the well known BPO companies are:

Genpact: Established in the year 1997, Genpact conducts a major portion of the outsourcing services in India. It offers outsourcing operations for big companies like GE Capital. Genpact has around 30 branches all across the globe and offers excellent services in the field of accounting and finance, customer service, insurance, analytics, IT infrastructure and so on. The company has staff strength of around 34,000 employees with revenue of around $822.7 million.

Daksh eServices: Ranking among the fastest growing BPO companies in India, Daksh has employee strength of around 5000. It offers high standard solutions in customer care and back office analytics. Some of the specialized departments include Technical Support, Customer Care, and Transaction Processes. In the year 2004, Daksh was taken over by IBM.

ICICI OneSource: ICICI OneSource specializes in providing solutions to various sectors such as healthcare, media, publishing, finance, and telecom. Recent surveys have shown that around 4500 people work in the company. The company has also received the BS 7799 certification.

EXL Services: EXL Services has its offices in Noida and Pune. It employs around 5000 employees and is a well known name among the BPO companies in India. It offers high quality services in mortgage lending, banking, health care, insurance, collections, and analytics. It has been awarded the prestigious ISO 9001:2000 certification for its quality performance.

HCL-Tech BPO: A subsidiary company of HCL Technologies, HCL-Tech BPO has around 3000 employees and offers cutting edge services in customer care, back office processing and so on. It has four centers in Bangalore, Chennai and Noida.